COLLECTED POEMS

Geoff Hattersley published and performed poetry from 1984. His work has been widely published and has been used as part of syllabuses in schools, universities, and with The Open University. He edited The Wide Skirt Press from 1986 until 1998, publishing 30 issues of the magazine and 24 books and pamphlets. He lived in Huddersfield with his wife Jeanette. Geoff passed away in 2024.

Also by Geoff Hattersley

Instead of an Alibi	(Broken Sleep Books, 2023)
Outside the Blue Hebium	(Smith Doorstop, 2012)
Back of Beyond	(Smith Doorstop, 2006)
Harmonica	(Wrecking Ball Press, 2003)
'On the Buses' with Dostoyevsky	(Bloodaxe Books, 1998)
Don't Worry	(Bloodaxe Books, 1994)
Port of Entry	(Littlewood Press, 1989)

CONTENTS

FOREWORD 7

DON'T WORRY 11
ON THE BUSES WITH DOSTOYEVSKY 135
HARMONICA 197
BACK OF BEYOND 271
OUTSIDE THE BLUE HEBIUM 385
INSTEAD OF AN ALIBI 419
WHAT NEV DID NEXT 495

GLOSSARY 517

© 2025, Geoff Hattersley. All rights reserved. No part of this book may be reproduced, stored in a retrieval system, or transmitted in any form or by any means, whether electronic, mechanical, photocopying, recording, or otherwise, without the prior written permission of the publisher, except in the case of brief quotations used in reviews or scholarly works.

This work may not be used for text and data mining, including (without limitation) the training of artificial intelligence technologies or systems. The author and publisher expressly reserve all rights and opt out of any applicable text and data mining exceptions.

ISBN: 978-1-917617-95-6

Cover designed by Aaron Kent

Edited and Typeset by Aaron Kent

The author has asserted their right to be identified as the author of this Work in accordance with the Copyright, Designs and Patents Act 1988

Broken Sleep Books Ltd
PO BOX 102
Llandysul
SA44 9BG

Collected Poems

Geoff Hattersley

Broken Sleep Books

FOREWORD

> There were 8 titles - mostly pamphlets - published between 1986 and 1990 and including "Port of Entry" - prior to "Don't Worry". They're listed in the front of Back of Beyond. The story begins with "Don't Worry" really though. I don't want "Port of Entry" or any of those other titles to be included.

This is what Geoff told me, when we began work on his *Collected Poems*. He had emailed me to tell me of his cancer diagnosis, and the prognosis, a couple of weeks before, but upon beginning work on this volume, he sprang into action. When discussing *Don't Worry*, his 1994 Bloodaxe release, Geoff said 'I think [Neil Astley] did a great job of representing the best of what was in those collections. He used approximately one third of the stuff. He used 13 from *Port of Entry*. Another third of that early work is absolute drivel and a complete embarrassment to me now. [...] The poems in those early titles show a young poet writing too much, certainly happier with what he'd written than he should have been, and finally finding a voice and way of expressing himself in parts two and three of *Don't Worry*.' Yet I felt like this was where I disagreed, Geoff hadn't written too much, in fact I felt he hadn't written enough. He had 4 full length collections in the thirty years between 1994 and 2024, boosted with a New and Selected, *Back of Beyond*, and a pamphlet, *Outside the Blue Hebium*. Geoff had a rare ability to write of the working-class struggle while inside it, and this gave his poetry both a sense of humour *and* an unflinching sense of reality. These poems truly were what was happening in the world when you dared to look outside of poetry for a moment.

'I'd like *Back of Beyond* to appear in its entirety.' Geoff continued. 'Although it uses a lot of poems from the three previously published books, many of them have been revised even if only slightly and it would be good for people to be able to see both versions and realise that I do actually work quite hard at trying to get my simple sounding stuff right.' And here is the problem with writing this foreword, trying to ensure the simplicity of Geoff's poetry is given the credit it deserves, because Geoff didn't just jot his poems down, he laboured over them, much in the way he laboured over the mould coming out of the LB350, or laboured on his hands and knees scrubbing the drains.

One thing to note is that these poems occasionally use terminology and language that is no longer considered appropriate or acceptable, and I spent a long time deciding whether to cut those poems, or censor those words, but ultimately decided Geoff isn't here to argue for or against their inclusion, and as such I only have that initial email to work from. I think it is key to note that when Geoff employs this language, it is never in praise of those words, but rather satirising, criticising, or admonishing those who find comfort in such terms. Likewise, Geoff is repeating and using the vernacular that was observed and heard around him.

In his last email about the collected volume, Geoff mentioned putting together a selection of new poems for the book, 'I want to try and put together a new collection to go at the end. [...] I'll see what I end up with, but that's what I'll be concentrating on to pass the time, and there's even a working title for the collection, which is *What Nev Did Next*.' Geoff's wife Jeanette found and posted these poems to me after Geoff's passing, and while it is great to have an account of what Nev did next, throughout this whole book what we're even more fortunate to have is What Geoff Did, and what Geoff did was remarkable.

— Aaron Kent,
May, 2025

Don't Worry

Bloodaxe, 1994

I. Because

BECAUSE

Because his face did not fit
he walked in sideways, on his hands,
pushing a wheelbarrow loaded with groceries.

His moustache sweating, he pogo-danced the bump
toward the bowl of tulips, grabbed a bunch
and ate them noisily while whistling 'Little Stevie'.

He gave piggy-back rides to all the pregnant women.
He impersonated a trout on the end of a hook.
He applauded their insults

because his face did not fit.
And if it's true he didn't 'get the joke',
it's also true the joke wasn't very funny.

THE CIGAR

The cigar was huge. It was carried in
by three underfed slave-children in chains.

Everything stopped: spoons on their paths to mouths,
hands and feet meeting knees beneath tables.

The American glanced around slowly,
the beginnings of an imbecilic grin…

Before the cartoon gapes of the other customers,
he summoned a blow-torch and lit the thing.

It began to expand at an alarming rate,
taking a new, strange form, developing

what seemed to be a head. One woman abandoned
her life's jewellery, collapsed to the ground moaning

'Give it *me*! Give it *me*!' Her husband, tears streaming,
gobbled a photograph of their lovely children.

Chandeliers fell crashing; in the darkness,
bottles of wine ran back to the cellar,

remarkable creatures leapt from their plates,
forked just in time by the sweating manager.

Waiters, their bow-ties on the verge of hysteria,
rushed to and fro with bowls of hot veal soup.

The American celebrated loudly
by eating the whole five-pound lump

of garlic stilton with port wine on the dessert trolley.
The room was small and becoming increasingly

smaller. There seemed no escape

BOYS' GRAMMAR SCHOOL:
THE NEW BOY HEARS GOOD ADVICE IN THE TOILET

Sing heartily the morning hymns
but remember: God

is a mathematics master
known, secretly, as Boris.

And God is with you;
always

bolt the door
when you smoke in the toilet

for remember: God
shall punish his errant children.

And you shall meet God
and tremble before Him.

And God shall frown
and God shall shout

and God shall slam His fist
upon the polished table-top.

And God's cane shall cut
through air and laws,

His hard-on no secret,
except to His wife.

FACTORY, LATE SEVENTIES

1. *Foreman*
The foreman requires
that things run smoothly.
His ambition is to be
world champion of foremen.
He paces the factory floor,
checking, checking, offering
words of encouragement
or abuse here and there.

I'm busy twisting the screwdriver
into the shining face
of the instrument panel
when he surprises me,
voice low in my ear:
'I could sack you for this…'
Then walks away, whistling.

2. *Knife*
Don leans forward,
lights my cigarette
with a match snapped in half
between finger and thumb,
tries to interest me again
in the NF: 'Our meetings
are dead inspiring.'
He has a loud voice
with which to call me
a dif and wog-lover
and believes I've no sense

of reality. I watch him
scratching PAKIS GO 'OME
on the toilet wall,
turning suddenly he says
'I always carry a knife,
didn't you know that?'

3. *Hand*
It's pie, chips and beans
again in the canteen
as Sukdhev shows me the hand
crushed in the machine
I'm working with now.
You must, he says, be careful.

Ralph overhears, tells me later
about the compensation –
the new car and central heating,
the softer job, swears
it's true: 'Half the blokes
in the place have at least
one finger missing, look
if you don't believe me.
Lose an arm, you hit the jackpot.'

All day I pull the pipes
out from the presses
just in time. It's automatic,
you can't go wrong, can't
just close your eyes and think
what you'll do with the money

SPLIT SHIFT

Everyone's reason
to smile: finished
for the day at two,

beer from ice-buckets
and music on the lawn
the whole afternoon.

I was working a split shift
in the kitchen, washing dishes
ten till two, five till eight.

The last thing I remember
is the sound of those dishes
hitting the ground outside

and the window,
one thin piece of glass
still tottering in the pane

like it's tempted
but can't quite allow
itself to fall.

THE JOKE

He's standing in the doorway
clutching his stomach.
He looks like any man
who's recently swallowed

a whole bottle of shaving foam
and doesn't know it.
We filled his mouth with it
last night at the party

after he'd fallen asleep
on the chair in the corner.
When we'd looked again, a little
later, the shaving foam

had gone, so we'd filled his mouth
again, and then again
till the bottle was empty.
It was a joke; we were all drunk.

Now in sunlight
he looks sadly at his stomach,
says he feels *a bit sick*,
and swears off alcohol.

SHADOWS ON THE BEACH

On the beach at Dahab, the sand was hot.
It felt good to sit there, to be naked
and take things easy, to glance out to where
the women plunged shouting into the sea.
On the radio, Jim Morrison wanted
to be loved two times, Ba-by, loved twice today.

A small Bedouin girl approached,
a shadow on the pages of my book.
I looked up, smiled. Shyly, she asked
if she could eat the apple-core
I'd just dropped in the sand.

NEW YEAR'S MORNING

I came to under a bush in the park.
My watch had stopped at half-one and the face
was cracked. There were sharp pains in my chest as
I mounted the gate to get out of there.

There were chip-papers, discarded, there were
discarded chips and contraceptives. I
wasn't sure which town or city it was.
Whose mind had cracked open to reveal those

high-rise flats? I dodged back and then ran as
the police-car stopped and the door opened.
I hid in a yard, could hear the coppers
no more than a few feet away shouting

Where are you, you little bastard? They soon
got bored though and gave it up. A headache
hit me then. It was a New Year, alright,
but the old were most certainly still in.

There are other stories from those days too.

LOVE POEM

Alan hates John and Pete.
Pete hates Alan and John.
John hates Pete but not Alan.
I hate Pete and Alan

and John. Alan hates me.
Pete and John might hate me
for all I know. Nev hates
no one. No one hates Nev, though

the two boys from Dover
hate the lot of us. We hate
the two boys from Dover.
The two girls from Finchley

hate John and would hate Alan
too if they knew he read
their diaries. We all hate
the people we see with

money, the people who buy
groceries. The people
hate us also. I hate
the smell of France and its wine.

THEOLOGY

A good friend of mine
one day; the next,
someone who just happened
to look like her.

'God tapped me on the shoulder'
she said
and handed me the leaflet.

Returning home on the bus
I heard one schoolgirl
telling another
'Simon Bletsoe put his hand
on my fanny last night.'

Later, the same one
tapped me on the shoulder
to ask for a light.

LOOMINGS, 1984

The future is a short journey by car
into a deep blue darkness –

such things will be common,
the pub comedians doing their best:

'A funny thing happened
on the way to Nottingham…'

I will be a broken radio
at the bottom of a filled-in mine-shaft,

all that will be left
of the village.

SHOULDERS

It was sad, as fathers and sons
who can't or won't speak
are sad, and I can't forget his face.

'No no no no'
was all he said, and then
'no no no no.'

He turned away
sharply and I stood
just a little behind

those broad, shaking shoulders,
useless
as a dead father to a live son.

MOON

The psychological need
for the drinking binge:
if you never let go,
how could you hold on?

Oh God give me the mind
of a moth, flying
inane circles
around my light-bulb,

give me the instincts
of an alligator, the humour
of a hyena, the anger
of a tea-drinking chimpanzee.

This is the quandary
of the young and foolish
as they begin to grow old:
there are, when you get down to it,

just two types of people alive,
those who have danced
beneath a full moon
and those who never have.

I would rather be a prisoner
than a prison-warder.
I would rather refuse a handout
than accept one.

I would like to live
at the bottom
of a swimming-pool,
the deep end.

HE WAS CERTAINLY AN INTELLECTUAL

He'd be there, poised with red pen
over the latest collection of Steiner essays,

eager to underline
everything obvious to you or me.

He liked to talk about famous literary figures:
Lawrence, Hardy, Eliot, Conrad, James —

they were all such wonderful people
who'd done such wonderful things.

He could talk for hours and hours.
Hadn't he written twenty-two hundred

letters over the years to *The Observer*?
Hadn't he read *Heart of Darkness*

seventeen times?
He could assure you he had.

THE NEW RIGHT

We tied him to a chair in a dark cellar
and pumped in water up to his chin.
After three days we drained the water
and revived him with a course of electric shocks.
> *For his own good.*

We removed his fingernails and teeth
and drilled holes in his face. He needed a meal
so we force-fed him rusty nuts and bolts.
We beat the soles of his feet with golf-clubs.
> *For his own good.*

We made him clean out the toilets with his beard.
We sawed off his left leg. He looked bored
so we hired a musician who entertained him
playing flute on his hollowed-out tibia.
> *For his own good.*

We put a live eel inside his anus and fed
his genitals to a rat. We stuck needles in his eyes.
We cut off his nipples with a pair of rose-clippers
and dipped his tongue in paraffin and set fire to it.
> *For his own good.*

With the aid of a suction-pump we removed his brain
through his ears and replaced it with mud.
We shot him at point-blank range five times
in the chest and six times in the head.
> *For his own good.*

SEX

I admit it freely:
I was sulky for a while,
turning up to parties
wearing the face Elvis sported
the day Priscilla slammed the door,

the face Nixon hid behind
in the summer of '73. Or
was it '74? Whichever,
there were some neat card-tricks
and a presidential pardon,

nonsense for posterity:
A new type of hairstyle
will be proposed at ten p.m.
Thank you, you may switch
off the tape machine.

Now I remember:
I was seventeen, a bad year
whatever face I pull at it,
my first job
leading to my second and third

and fourth, none of them
anything
but spit on the head.
Then there was the sex thing.
We don't talk about sex.

THAT WEEKEND, YOU WORE

a tragic expression and were
loaded with meaningful glances.

We walked along the beach whipped
by sand on the wind, poked
at crabs half-eaten by gulls

and later, on the boating lake,
lost the oars and were forced
to abandon ship in the high wind.

There had to be a toilet
somewhere, but we couldn't find it,
so you disappeared into a bush,

and an old man's eyes grew wide
as he hobbled by—my clothes
dripping wet, a bent fag in my lips,

murmuring sweet nothings to a bush.

PORTRAIT

'God I just love
your face' she says.

I'm sitting still
as she draws me,

trying to think
of something other

than how my arse
is killing me.

'Be patient your face
is a bastard

God I love it
I just love it!'

When the portrait
is done I might

carry it with me
in an inside

jacket pocket,
looking at it

occasionally
to see who I am.

MUCKY

She puts down the magazine
and says she needs a bath,
looking at me as though
I do too or perhaps
only wanting me there with her

whether I'm mucky or not.
She's read 'The Platonic Blow'
(attributed to Auden)
just now and shows the face
that makes me grin and want

to hold her and startle her
with something of my own.
How mucky could I be? I
wonder, as the water
flows and the mirror steams.

SHEEP'S BRAIN

She tells me she once ate
a sheep's brain—now

here's me, with my tongue
halfway down her throat.

HALF-TIME

My main concern for the moment is me,
how I know food without sniffing at it,
know newspapers without picking them up,
how I can't even say the word *bathroom*
in anything other than a whisper.

Don't tell me it's not real, all that stuff
about heroic flights to distant stars
and pressing the ejector-button *just in time*.
It's real as this plate of chips, this sausage.
My best friends are all unemployable.

HOURS

They drove the tanks over the barricades
and shot at anything moving
and I remembered:
A smoked mackerel salad
must be prepared for six o'clock.

Hours became neat words
and acts of love
and they poked long batons
into the prisoners' gunshot wounds
causing them to scream constantly.

FRANK O'HARA FIVE, GEOFFREY CHAUCER NIL

I think on the whole I would rather read
Frank O'Hara than Geoffrey Chaucer, and
this fine, non-smoking morning could well be
the right time to try out a new (uh hum)

poetic form. It's the funniest thing:
I am *here*, thirty years of age, having
put booze and all sorts of, say, 'dubious
substances' behind me, now sweating it

all out in a small, constipated room
with a plump tomato of a woman,
conjugating Middle English verbs. I have
developed a line, a very brief line,

in gestures of friendliness, and in my
trousers an idea is taking shape.

CARTE BLANCHE

Am I a person given to buffoonery?
A foolish jester? In short, a half-wit?

Am I a poor clown, awkwardly mimicking
the chief clowns in shows? Am I Merry Andrew?

These days my life is a sales campaign
conducted from a position of severe disadvantage

and the whole world's ambition
is to offer me shitty advice.

The only words I can think of
to describe my situation

are 'zany'
and 'sleep-needy'

and they are the wrong words—
believe me, Mac! 'Zany'

and 'sleep-needy'
are completely the wrong words.

I'M PUTTING ON WEIGHT, LAST YEAR'S TROUSERS

I give to my younger brother. He makes
some witty remark concerning those old
Orson Welles' wine adverts, and I tell him
Orson had been a genius, once, too.
Meanwhile, I suppose my ambition
(if I'm to be honest about it) is
to be paid to make those adverts. Fat chance.

WITHIN THESE WALLS

The revolution is but
a matter of days away
and dust settles on my
shelves and sleeping cat.
I'm a hundred miles from
where I was last week yet
this seat I'm sitting in looks
for all the world like
the same seat. Yesterday
I told my parents I'd
found a job and they
thought it a joke. It
was. The self-portrait
I have daubed, I call
'Still Life'.

WORKSONGS

Sober at last,
and on a day like this.
But to go back to what
I was saying last night:
Would you kill the bosses,
given half a chance
and a cast-iron alibi?

*

The woman in the canteen
saw me from a passing bus
at the crossroads in Bradley
on Saturday with my wife.
She holds up an almost
empty jar of Nescafé
like it was a death threat—
'I only bought it yesterday,
it cost four pounds thirty-nine.'
The first cup of the day is free.

*

I'm in charge
of my own room
the others in it
do as I say,
if they know what's

Actually, they do
as they like,

which suits me fine,
though the boss
takes me aside:
'You're in charge
of this room, this machine.
Lay the law down,
lay the bloody
law down.'

*

The machine won't work
and I must make it.
I know less about it
than I do the temperature of rocks
in the Negev desert.
I know less about it
than I do the psychological needs
of tropical fish.
'What's the problem?'
the boss asks, poking
his nose round the door.
'The water molleton roller,
it needs replacing.'
It ought to fool him
at least another week.

*

The machine, the machine,
the bloody machine.
If I close my eyes

I see the machine.
If I open my eyes
I see the machine.
If I lick my lips
I taste the machine.

*

To call this living
is to call the ceiling sky,
the bathtub ocean.

At the end of each shift
and when I arrive the next morning
the place still stands.

I clear my head
of everything but the job,
decide the day's goal.

This day
that could have gone
anywhere.

CHRISTMAS SHOPPING, SHEFFIELD

You were writing dud cheques
like no one's business,
I was splashing
the forged tenners around.

In the Hole in the Road
someone sang
'Take Me To Tulsa',
snow settling on his sombrero.
I tossed him a tenner
screwed into a ball.

A woman approached
armed with documents
and truth;
she was selling badges,
a definite bargain
at a tenner apiece.

I signed the petition
to end Apartheid,
I do a lot
of possibly useless writing.

IT'S SUNDAY

The man across the road
paints his drain-pipe bright red

while his wife holds the ladder
and Jimmy Saville recalls 1982

in short blurts of sap
that run into each other

to form one long blurt.
The corners of his mouth

dripping from the edge of his chin
the old boy next door

hands me a letter marked URGENT
delivered by mistake to him

three months ago.
Someone starts to mow his lawn

and then a couple of others
put on their oldest clothes too

and it's like a benevolent mental disease:
pretty soon, half the neighbourhood

are mowing their lawns in the sunshine
that glints blandly on row upon row

of identical rooftops and windows.

THE MAN AT NUMBER TEN

slams his front door:

there goes a man who
takes himself seriously,

shoulders hunched
for passers-by,

always busy
going nowhere, fast.

He spends every Sunday
with his head in an engine

and every single evening
throwing darts at a board.

He seems content
with a dog and a wife

and I've sometimes seen him
take one or both for a walk.

ALMOST UNBELIEVABLY

Sad, to be sitting here still
smoking too many cigarettes,
watching this cold pancake of a film
for the third time in one life,

to consider my mother,
patiently sitting through Western
after Western with my father
because she *liked the scenery*.

History repeats itself, after
a fashion, and these also
are facts: the diaries we've kept
would make appropriate palimpsests,

our stamp collection
ranks among the dull.
When the toast caught fire
last night and the grill,

it was the most exciting event
here for at least three years.

FUTURE GAMES
for Peter Sansom

In summer and autumn
the kids spent the evenings

racing skateboards downhill
to the river. Now in winter

they find pleasure or pain indoors.
The suits their dads go drinking in,

the cars left standing in the rain,
show the sort of money

available—what seems
a never-ending pile.

Soon they'll make a sort of progress,
shuffling to interviews

that will become concerns,
jokes told over half-pints

that will last half the night—
as the glasses empty

they will too, into years
that get harder.

They won't ever feel powerful,
won't be.

They'll fit locks and raise dogs
to keep each other out,

they'll watch the river get
dirtier, deadlier.

They'll stop and gawp
at the sculpture

in memory
of the swimmers of '96.

Ear and throat infections
will be common killers.

SINGING

Everybody's singing, they call it that.
In the bath, in the kitchen, in the car
on the way to work. And what do they sing?

They sing, Ooh Ba-by, let me feel your love.
They sing, Ooh Ba-by, need your-las-tic-lips.
They sing, Ain't ea-sy for no man a-lone.

Everyone, in their cars, bathrooms, kitchens—
singing, singing. This is happiness, here.

THE DRUMMER

He claimed to be a drummer
just a drummer

though we couldn't help but notice
the sticks in his hands, the obscenity

the way he'd stare, stare
ahead as he drummed

disturbing with his drums
his *drumming* the neighbourhood

stirring up things, things
best left unstirred, yes

at times *directly polemical*
this this this this drummer.

We could break his hands
and we did break them.

BRIEFCASE

Life makes as much sense to me
as a ripe avocado does to a dog:
I was passed an unsigned cheque
by a man impersonating a friend

and got back home to a cold meal.
I found a man's black leather briefcase
in the corner of the bedroom
and knew it was my own.

HOW SHE PUTS IT

'It's about time you grew up' she says,
as though he doesn't know that theory.

'All I said' he starts to say
but she's not interested

in all he said, slamming
the door as she leaves.

He's both feet on her coffee table
when she later tells him it's over:

'Get out and take your ugliness with you'
is how she puts it.

THE SAXOPHONIST'S EYES

turn to the
doorway slowly

where two old drunks
are denying everything

then back to where
they found the music.

One drunk spills
his false teeth:

a quick wipe on a leg
they're in again.

SCARED

He knows he's done wrong but wrong was done to him too.
In the first place his father read *The Lone Ranger*
to him each night as he masturbated.
His penis loathed itself. All his classmates
used to hang their coats and caps on his hook.

It didn't stop there. His first gun back-fired.
He was trying, it's true, to kill himself.
The woman happened to be in the way.
Then he got scared and things got out of hand.
The plane leaves in one hour thirty minutes.

DESERT

We were out in the desert, just sort of
fooling around, dreaming up names for some
loud, long-haired rock band we'd be sure to form
the minute we got back home. I liked most

Doctor Straight Neck and his Toothpick Killers.
That was when Heidi started laughing and
couldn't stop—as much the drink and heat as
the wit, I guess. But it was good, hearing

her laugh like that, after the rape and all.
The desert could do that. Such stillness there,
as if the earth was taking breath, as if
history was yet to be invented.

I look after cacti in the house now.
They don't take much of that. I never did
keep in touch with any of those people,
though I heard Heidi died in Berlin, smack.

SNOWBALLS, ITALY

The Italians had received a tip-off:
on the border with France
a long line of traffic stretched back

through the deep, still-falling snow
like a black studded belt
across folds of white flesh.

I was sweating things out on the bus
among tattooed French and Dutch racists
when torchlight shook me up further.

We stood shivering by the road-side
as they emptied our bags brusquely one by one.
I needed a bath, I think people could tell.

As we left in the poor light
I watched young, bullet-shaped policemen
throwing snowballs at each other, laughing.

SPIDER

The spider was completely unprepared
for assault from above by an ash-tray,
it never had a friend it could count on.
It never knew its blood-group.
It never saw itself changing, or any need to.
It never said: 'No more excuses.'
It never felt tempted by drugs.
It never knew the itch to the nearest bar.
Its earning power was never an issue.
It was never hurt by a few home-truths.
It never did anything for anyone.
It never knew the myth of Wyatt Earp.
It never hoped for more than was likely.
It never had Watchtower thrust at it.
It never saw a rainbow, or a bunch of flowers
dropped into an open grave.
It never wrote an essay on the works of Alexander Pope.
It never filled in an application form.
It never married for love or money.
It never had a honeymoon in a hotel.
It never knew who was Prime Minister.
It never knew if it was lucky or not.
It never shopped for clothes.
It never smiled.
It never felt like a paperclip
in a jar in a cupboard in a shed.
It never carried a briefcase.
It never missed the last train.
It never slept off a hangover.
It never thought it was Marlon Brando.

It never grew a beard, or shaved in cold water.
It never fished in the Mississippi.
It never heard rumours about itself.
It never had to face its inadequacy.
It never had any wild ideas.
It never had any wild ideas drummed out of it.
It never laughed at a copper's helmet.
It never gave a false name and address.
It never saw The Marx Brothers, or listened to Sgt. Pepper.
It never knew what was in fashion.
It never got careless, or said it was past caring.
It never left its clothes lying in a heap.
It never preferred to remain anonymous.
It never wondered who wrote Shakespeare
or invented light-bulbs.
It never thought it would win an award one day.
It never moved because it didn't like the neighbourhood.
It never fastened its seat-belt for a rough ride.
It never played a guitar that had just one string.
It never looked for warts in its armpits.
It never turned its back on the dreams of its youth.
It never felt guilty for wasting time.
It never considered circumcision.
It never got hard-ons travelling by bus.
It never got sentimental at Christmas.
It never thought the carpet and curtains clashed.
It never spent a night awake with its partner
wishing the photograph album empty.
It never read about itself on the front page.
It never had more than its fair share of problems.
It was never diagnosed manic-depressive.
It was never found guilty of a thing.

It never made a list of things to do.
It never waited for the right partner to come along,
or became half of a couple with a headache between them.
It never dropped earwax in the ashtray.
It never had a first at the races.
It never tied a donkey to someone sleeping.
It never had a pension plan.
It never wanted to impress itself,
or thought it was better than it was.
It never got serious over the funniest things.
It never had a boss for a friend,
or a friend who thought he was a boss.
It never stared out to sea, it never watched the tide come in.
It never worried whether or not it created a good impression.
It never took notice of a roadsign.
It never put a barbed-wire fence up.
It never wept inside headphones, briefly.
It never learned to think things over more,
to peep before it plunged.
It never took its shoes off to save the carpet.
It never learned to spell archaeologist.
It never scratched its arse in a food-queue.
It never read a book about Hitler.
It never met a neo-oligarch.
It never used washing powder, or learned to start a fire.
It never used a telephone-box.
It never accepted a cigarette.
It never laughed at its own joke.
It never sat in the back row,
or dreamt it was the steering-wheel through James Dean's chest.
It never grew its hair to its shoulders.
It never picked its feet on the bed.

It never had a twenty-first birthday party.
It never washed its hands of anybody.
It never needed an explanation, or a diet.
It never said: 'Too gentle for my liking, too jolly.'
It never taught itself German, telling its partner
to be quiet so it could concentrate.
It never worried about what it was swallowing.
It never looked for heroes and villains.
It never smiled apologetically.
It never pressed a blade into its wrist.
It never wished it lived in a caravan.
It never fried bacon and eggs.
It never felt like a fat catalogue
of books published in limited editions
no one wants anyhow, not at any price.
It never tore a book in half.
It never felt like it was an abstract
that has everybody shaking their heads.
It never had a gun held to its head.
It never felt a wire tightened round its throat.
It was completely unprepared
for assault from above by an ashtray.
I should blush and compose
a relevant soundtrack for that moment.

II. ACT

ACT

It was a normal day, raining
as he walked to the off-licence,
and there wasn't a bone in his body
someone wouldn't like to break
like a twig beneath the wheels of a slow train
or like a boiled egg brought down hard on a steel plate.

He'd thought his act had been simple;
clearly it hadn't been simple enough.
It's true some of the jokes were in bad taste
('the headless French horn player' springs to mind)
and some were hardly jokes at all—at least,
there's no point telling them if people can't get them.

One thing: he'd found out who his friends weren't.
He wouldn't want it any other way.

They'd packed him into a small suitcase.
What hadn't fit had been left at the station.

SLAUGHTERHOUSE

At last, I was ready to say goodbye
to a tether made of fishnet stockings.
My friends told me not to, that I needed
a bandage for my head, needed a crutch for it.
I muttered Jolly Good like a jolly fellow,
caught the next bus. When I got where it was going
a man tried to sell me a Coke for five dollars.
I asked the next for the way to the slaughterhouse.
He told me to follow the smell of meat and bone.
The smell was powerful, at some distance even.

*

The first time I ate grilled octopus tentacles
– a strange moment, one I feel a need to mention.
An undercover cop had leeched onto me at a bar,
between mouthfuls of ouzo and tentacles
was pretending to be the greatest punk rock band ever.
He asked if I wanted to dance, the meathook
in my hand was reassuring. He loved every minute
of his pathetic life. Young men with sticks
surrounded our piled-high table
after he told the barman he should fuck his bill.

*

The morning after I ate grilled octopus tentacles
a man helped me buy powder in the pharmacy,
took me by the arm and found me a hotel room.
I was embarrassed among strangers the rest of the day—

they were passing round photos taken on the beach
that summer I weighed fifteen and a half stone.
At night I searched every room in the place,
sifting through bins stuffed with used tampons and shit-roll
for one small thing that would let me know where I was.
The landlady joined me about half-two.

*

I did press-ups and pull-ups and ran on the spot.
I brushed my teeth and shaved away three months
of enthusiastic cunnilingus.
I practised speaking without using shit and fuck
and held myself erect. Bumping into her on the stairs
I complimented her on her repertoire
but suggested she make more of a noise.
What do I most wish now, as I pick my teeth here
some years later? That she had understood a word I said
and that my nose hadn't been so obviously running.

*

The slaughterhouse started my head pounding
and there is a harsh sound, a hundred cows
screaming in unison. I went nuts there
and then. Years of treatment would have followed
if I hadn't escaped the building that minute.
I hitched a lift with a man who told me
I had good legs, sexy legs. He needed glasses
and a room at a hotel, I replied
– did he have his wallet? Yes he did. His head cracked
as he landed in the road, I didn't look back.

*

What I fell in love with was her singing,
not that it was what you'd call good singing.
It would reach me in my room as I lay naked
in the baked afternoons, talking aloud
to the insects on the ceiling and walls.
It was the happiness that surprised me,
and how it lingered a long time after.
I was never a music critic, no,
Not bad, I'd say, turning this way and that,
looking in the mirror at my pale face.

UNTITLED, KIBBUTZ, LATE SEVENTIES

He went round the dining room collecting
the unfinished bottles of sabbath wine
like a parody of Chaplin's drunken waiter
with a tray he somehow balanced just right.
And drank three half-pint glasses of vodka

and three bottles of beer in six minutes.
And collapsed, people dancing over him
as if he was a discarded jacket.
Then found himself acting the lumberjack,
singing at the top of his voice as the trees fell.

The Committee decided he wasn't dangerous
but resolved to keep a close watch on him.
He felt like he was a new species at a zoo.
He turned up to dinner disguised as Yasser Arafat,
reappeared the next day at the wedding party

as a rabbi who went round sniffing pants,
peeing where he felt like it, in front of the bride even,
and terrorised elderly guests
throughout the night, marching along their porches,
all Hitler moustache, goose-steps and salutes.

The Committee decided to give him a chance, another one.
He felt like he was bleeding to death in a stadium
with a capacity crowd having paid to watch.
He went to work with a swastika inked on his forehead.
He attacked a crippled war hero with a sweeping brush.
The Committee decided he deserved a chance.

THE FAT MAN IN PARIS

In the cafés and bars are all my friends.
I'm paying for all the drinks, everything.
What do I need money for if not friends?
What do I need friends for? There is no friend:
I've been through it, she says, I've had enough.

Let me tell you about the man who watches me.
He's sipping water at the bar in Jamaica.
He's on the beach in his suit in Miami.
Now we're in Paris; he watches, follows.
He knows I know, wants me to know.

A lizard by the bathroom door
stares as I dress. The girl's dressed already.
Take the whole five hundred, I say,
you've earned it. She says, God knows that.
I stop dressing and she leaves quietly.

Stinking leather boots, stinking leather pants.
I phone California, wanting to talk.
Needing to, but it's hard, it's John.
I am bloated, ugly, friendless, dying,
filling the bath with my vomit and unguents.

The man who watches me, who follows me,
he's across the road from the telephone,
he's talking with Customs at the airport.
He's running to keep up with the taxi,
taking it in his stride like a soldier.

The weight on my chest, the noise in my head.
Please god fuck my head for good completely.
Paris is an open prison, clever, clever.
The human race is one pair of scared eyes.
I see it coming, embrace it, so cold.

PIECES FOR THREE WOODEN BLOCKS

1

He won't go out the house
if a car's parked in front of it.
Instead he skulks in the cellar
where a pan collects rainwater
which he pours down the sink
each morning. He wears dark glasses
the whole time, even when shaving
in the mirror that needs cleaning.
A radio programme has to be taped
but there's no one he can trust to do it.

2

He sits quiet as an empty umbrella-stand.
He's closed the curtains and left the lights off.

He knows his enemies won't let it drop:
They'll stick his head on a pole, dance round it.

He's closed the curtains and left the lights off.
He thinks of a room with a door with no handle.

*

They'll stick his head on a pole, dance round it.
He should have listened to what friends told him.

He thinks of a room with a door with no handle.
He'd like that room. He'd like that door a lot.

He should have listened to what friends told him:
You go there with that face you can expect trouble.

*

He'd like that room, he'd like that door. A lot.
The thing he just can't get out of his head's

You go there with that face you can expect trouble.
Nothing's a joke, nothing's funny, nothing.

The thing he just can't get out of his head's
he knows his enemies won't let it drop.

Nothing's a joke, nothing's funny, nothing.
He sits quiet as an empty umbrella-stand.

3

He wondered what he'd see outside the car
and not from the seat where his legs were limp,
as though he'd walked a great distance or up
some flights of stairs, his thighs aching. He looked
out at the men and women, the women
more than the men, the way they stood, heads back
at the roadside. It seemed less of an illusion
now it was no longer what he'd see. What he'd see
too soon and for ever was something else.
He didn't want his eyes to water, but they did.

THE BOOTLEG SERIES

He was still raving about Dylan's
The Bootleg Series months later.
He'd had his season in Hell
though the devil still visited
from time to time in the form
of sounds from the street.

His ex would call on Saturdays,
drop off their daughter. He'd play
The Bootleg Series and try
to get Christine to eat something.
She was between one and a half and two.
It's a funny age to be,

a funny one to watch.
She cheered him up when the grilling
he'd had from the detectives
started to get him down,
remembering the ice-bath.
The Bootleg Series cheered him up too.

The Bootleg Series was playing
the day the lawyer's letter came
telling him to forget it,
he was in poverty and would be
as long as his name wasn't
formerly Robert Allen Zimmerman,

The Bootleg Series his latest release,
bringing together strands

from a brilliant thirty-year career—
Christine could even dance
to parts of it, danced her dolls too
and joined in here and there.

So he traded in his mouth organ
for a fountain pen and got a job
writing job applications for people
who couldn't write their own
for some reason. He'd have gone nuts
if it wasn't for *The Bootleg Series*.

The year went past uneventfully.
His nails grew again,
his only pleasures in life
were *The Bootleg Series* and beer.
He put a little weight on,
took lessons in opening his mouth

without offending someone.
Christmas was a bastard of course,
but by the New Year he was
fully re-charged, ready to move.
He packed *The Bootleg Series*,
took a boat and finished up

eating pizza at a table
by the Med. *The Bootleg Series*
found new fans in the soldiers
who visited him in the room
where he cut the deals. He made
a killing and got out quick,

bought a house with the profits
in the remotest place he could think of.
Things drifted in and out of favour,
he found God, then lost Him,
but never at any point stopped
listening to *The Bootleg Series*.

YOU'RE NOT EVEN FUNNY, NOT EVEN SMART

Responsibilities, I collect them,
trying to bring you to your senses my latest.
Nobody knows what you've been through
and you'll keep it to yourself a while yet.
You sweat behind the bolted door, the cops
have twenty guns pointing at it, you've got
to open it, walk out. You finger your rifle
and weigh up the options and there are none.
Come in, you say, I've been expecting you.

Like I'm trapped in a phone box with a smell
I stand in your room and think *money back*.
You kick out your leg and the door closes
like a ton of rock, like a thousand tons.
You sit down, cross your feet at the ankles.
Sit down, you say, indicating a stool.
I think how sick you look, how very sick
as you suck that thermometer, dribbling.
You aren't dead but your room smells worse than it ought to.

You wanted all the things you thought you'd never want.
And stood aside, like a cardboard figure
let the other man push right in, the one
with bacon fat sticking to his front teeth.
He loved winding you up, you're so easy.
You're not even funny, not even smart
he told you in the rain, and he was right.
You're as good as dead, already buried, he said.
There's one in every town, you're it in ours.

How was it? Their endearments made you sick,
the love-making all but finished you off?
You shouldn't have been under the mattress.
I've read your notes, they're daft, obscene.
I don't know what you expected.
Now you tell yourself you don't care
and the funny thing is you don't, do you?
I look at your petulant mouth
and want to drag you outside by the hair.

PROBLEMS WITH THE OVERFLOW

You don't like to lose your cool and you don't
often. If you do, you think of a machine
that moves through the streets chopping legs off at the knees
and now the kids on the corner whistle
the funeral procession as you pass them.
But you're pretty thick-skinned and can take it
and there's always something to keep you from brooding:
a door that won't open or a door that won't close,
an overflow that keeps overflowing
or signs of strength or weakness in a rival.
What do you care if someone else freezes
in a bath they should have emptied?
You listened through the wall as he sang: he was deep
as a country 'n' western compilation
and with the same belief in the double-negative,
crackling like a 78 when he should have been a CD.
If his future was a building it would be demolished
but it's nothing to you since you woke up
and lit a fire — not a large one, about
the size of a copper's helmet or head.

Not far from where you spit, a family play
croquet on the lawn. There's a bright steel skateboard
poking under their gate like a machine.

DOMESTIC

A shame the windows jammed, so the house smells
of paint and turps, some other stuff. But it looks great
from the end of the path or the end of the street.
You feel pleased with yourself, your guests can tell.
And they're glad to see you've got your sense of humour

back from the drycleaners. It's called taste, you tell them,
opening the wine, moving from person to person,
each one placed round the table in the right order.
You've gone to great lengths, *The Sultans of Swing*
insinuating. And then suddenly

your sister turns up without her husband, crying.
He's the most selfish prick she's ever known, she says.
You haven't seen her for five years, and here she is.
You say what you've always thought: 'Yes, you're right, he is.'
'Oh you rotten bastard' she says and leaves.

Your guests don't mention it, but something's changed.
Soon there's a strained atmosphere which even
your most highly-prized two-liners can't dispel.
One in the bush is worth two in the hand
if it's the right bush, you say. Everyone gapes.

Midnight, you sit in your kitchen and weep.
Your wife weeps too, but you don't comfort each other.

FOREVER CHANGED

You're tired, running a temperature, carrying
your empty medicine bottles to the dustbin.
The man you used to call dad hides behind it,
 leaps out, boots you in the balls and face,
tips a bucket of piss over your head.
This happens every day, you're never ready.

Then you lose your job and all your savings
on a stupid bet. Your wife packs her bags,
takes the kids, moves to another country.
She's drilled holes in the radiators,
trampled avocados into the carpets
and warped your entire record collection.

The next thing you know you're beat up
and arrested in a dawn raid, charged with
possession of narcotics and firearms
and assaulting a police officer.
You're innocent but no one believes you.
Your lawyer washes his hands of you,

someone nails your cat to the door. Suddenly
you're getting letters of abuse, death-threats,
gift-wrapped substances that sting your fingers.
The postman tells you he hates you,
the milkman refuses to leave you milk,
people turn up to laugh and jeer at you

in the hairdresser's and supermarket,
follow you down the street throwing bottles
and rocks, dogs snapping at your heels.

The man you used to call dad kills himself,
leaves a note blaming you. Your novel
is dismissed as the ravings of a sick man.

Then every lover you've had publishes memoirs
in the Sunday papers, the details are awful.
Tuesday, you're photographed in a nightclub
with two fourteen-year-old girls and described
as a kinky pervert, a corrupter of youth,
a collector of soiled knickers.

Then your house is destroyed by fire.
Everything's gone, you don't even have one
photo of your kids' birthday parties left.
Your terrapins were boiled alive.
Your mother was asleep in the spare room.
Your wife hadn't renewed the insurance.

You wake in the night in a cheap hotel
to find you're deaf in your left ear,
have gone bald and have an ache
in the only two teeth you still bite with.
Then you're sitting at a bar looking scared.
A good Samaritan moves in to finish it.

MINUS THREE POINT SIX

Suppose there are three doors:
Religion, Insanity, Suicide.
Suppose you're on TV,
the hostess asks which door you'll take.
Suppose ten million viewers

and a studio audience of enemies
are all shouting their preference
and in the din the hostess mishears:
you ask for Religion, get Insanity.
You're shoved through and the door closes.

You try to shout for help, you want
to explain there's been a mistake,
you can't, can't move, feel as if
you're held in place by chains
or a pair of huge hands.

It's so dark you can't see yourself,
so quiet you could hear a plant move
though there are none moving.
There are no words in your head, just numbers.
You try but can't stop thinking about them:

One and one is two plus seventeen is eighteen
minus three point six is fifteen point eight
multiplied by twenty-seven point seven is
four thousand three hundred and sixty-five point six
divided by five point five is

FINGERPRINTS

You hate the way the light-shade casts shadows
from a clear bulb. And now shiny black book covers
that pick up fingerprints. All you can smell
is boot polish and uniforms, the ink
on a statement you're supposed to have made.
You don't believe you said a word of it.
The door gets further away and isn't opened.

You're such a let-down, don't say the right things.
You wish you weren't who you are, aren't sure who.
There's a long line of men holding batons.
They'll rip your bollocks off, make you eat them.
They'll go at you till you believe everything
they tell you, you're the lowest of the low.
The door gets further away and isn't opened.

You crouch in the corner as the room shrinks
to the size of a crushed kneecap, small but
large enough to stick in your throat
from where a sound emerges, something like
a half-hearted prayer at a graveside
mixed with the sobs of genuine mourning.
The door gets further away and isn't opened.

PATHOLOGICAL

The director won't get out of his chair,
the caravan door's locked. Someone
knocks and asks if he's ready yet
two or three times an hour. There are
helicopters waiting, the police

have sealed off all the roads.
Leave me alone, the director whispers.
The last stages of something terminal
are all over the scene when he shoots it
three identical days later.

Government men follow him everywhere,
there's no hiding place. He crouches
in the shower, chanting. The water's
turned on full, his clothes are soaking.
He's trying to spot the microphone.

He goes for a paper, doesn't get back
for twelve weeks, can't say
where he's been. Doesn't know
a thing about it. He's twitching
like the beginning of a movie.

Keeping quiet like he's holding back
something big. No one suspects
his thoughts are of nothing.
He can shoot an apple off someone's head
or miss and not care less.

A HOUSE WITH BARE FLOORBOARDS

You peep through the upstairs window,
trying to figure out how much they know
behind the fence at the bottom of the garden.
You feel, you say, like a small child
is asking you questions in another language.

You've a tape that plays backwards
and sounds better that way, some apples
in a wooden basket: red, green, rotten.
I should ask why you took
the carpets up, cut them into pieces

about the size of table-mats,
crammed them inside plastic containers
and put them on the kitchen shelves.
Bare wood against bare feet, you say,
think I'll grow my sideburns again.

For a while now you've been well out of it,
believing in the existence of ghosts,
hardly daring to breathe or show your face.
It's good to have all that cleared up, you say,
to know the facts and nothing else.
You feel like laughing in the street
but don't want to make another mistake.

Now you're frowning, trying to remember
where you left your brown overcoat, afraid
you could have misplaced it for good.

HANNON IN A NUTSHELL

His gripe was with the whole world, everyone,
and it seemed no amount of money
would put a smile on that long face.
His seventh album, called *Seventh Album*,
bristled with unresolved grievances,
'The Big Ships' and 'On The Other Hand'
the tracks that attracted most attention.
In the former, a solitary piano chord
repeated at five-second intervals
as Hannon grunted his ex-wife's name
was the sparest rock recording
since the heyday of Eight Nipples With An Attitude.
'On The Other Hand', on the other hand,
was its antithesis, a wild incantation
positively celebrating his loneliness,
the twenty-five percussionists
taking it into uncharted territory.
It is a stunning performance, shocking
as an amputation, twisted even, perhaps
completely paranoid, quite psychotic.

Hannon's mental decline over the following years
is well-documented elsewhere. Suffice to say
the Nixon Holiday Inn disturbance
was not an isolated incident
and the artistic output suffered correspondingly.
His relevance to the young of today
can be summed up thus: there but for the grace of God
could have gone your dad.

THREE MORNINGS

You're waiting for the post,
nothing else is happening.
When it fails to arrive
you make a series of tapes,
your hundred favourite songs
by a hundred different artists.
It passes some twelve hours,

another seven and a half
listening back. By then
it's the morning, you're hanging on
for the post again, tired
but not sleepy. And surprised
how dull the songs sounded
the second time.

You apply for a job:
Head of Comedy
in a run-down comprehensive.
It goes to someone
who looks like Edgar Allan Poe
pretending to be Herman Melville,
a party-pooper for sure.

Then you're eating a pile
of toast. You watch
the postman walk past.
He's the same party-pooper
you saw in the dream.
His hair's a little
different, somehow.

NOBEL PRIZE POEM

He awoke with no hangover
because he'd had no beer
and looked in the mirror.
He couldn't help noticing
that a box of old records
not worth listening to
teetered on his neck
in place of a head.
He tied his shoelaces.
He was barefoot.

*

At the time, he was seeing
a Scandinavian woman
whose life was her watercolours:
orange skies, pink highways.
She wanted to live in a cave
and win the Nobel Prize.
I'm not interested
in saving the world, he told her,
it's hard enough remembering
to change my underpants.

*

Then he wrote a story
about a bad writer
and thirty-seven people
sent him insulting letters:

How dare he portray them
in such a callous manner?
He couldn't even remember
meeting fourteen of them.
Three or four of them
were actually good writers.

GREY

It's not surprising he's gone a little grey
from the events of the past year or two,

only that he's not gone completely bald,
and he still can't believe he was ever

ridiculous enough to fall in love with her.
She turned him into the sort of man

who takes a packet of ham sandwiches
to work in a briefcase, one who sneers on the bus;

a man who feels like a book no one publishes
or an event history doesn't record.

*

She's like the knife-thrower's calm assistant,
she knows this much at least about the place she's in:

It's better than being buried up to your neck
with a bag of snakes tied over your head.

Her husband sounds completely furious,
something about his childhood and *it's not funny*.

She's noticed he laughs at different things.
In fact, he rarely laughs at anything

and this more than anything makes her laugh.
She starts after he leaves the room.

THE LAST TIME I SAW ERNEST HEMINGWAY

he told me all bad writers were in love
with the epic, punching me in the ribs.
It was the sort of thing I'd got used to
after the twelfth drink. This was the same night

Steinbeck dropped in to introduce himself.
'No chin son of a bitch' Ernest shouted,
'I'm a better goddamn writer than you…'
and bit the neck off a whiskey bottle.

In some biographies, he breaks a stool
over his head as well, but I was there
and this didn't happen—so much that's said
about him's bull. Something not so well known

is that the CIA were onto him
for supporting Castro. 'That's one' he said,
pointing to some squarehead drinking tonic,
and for the first time in our long friendship

I knew Ernest Hemingway was frightened.

STAR GUEST OF THE DAY

Everybody's laughing
about this comedian

who's been found guilty
of blackmailing himself,

though I prefer his
semi-serious roles,

like *Jackson*, who trims
his wife's pubic hair,

suggests she puts it
in a pie for him.

He was also good in
A Pile of Babies

And A Pile of Sand,
where he tells Cockwormer,

the bookmaker who loves him,
'They wish they had my head

in a noose. They have. My legs
are starting to tremble

like a house For Sale board
in a hard wind.' His face

is a blank domino under a table
among a group of boots that need polishing.

EYES, LIPS, MISS

He was out of his head for a long time,
moving from place to place, making few friends,

behaving like a minor character
in an unwritten country 'n' western number.

These days he hardly goes out of the house.
He's got everything he needs right with him.

He flicks through photographs of his ex-wife,
chooses the prettiest, pins it to the dartboard.

He hasn't rinsed his coffee cups in years.
He throws the darts: nose, eye, miss, chin, miss, eye

FIVE YEARS

Easy to see what had gone against him
now it was finished. He'd sit in the dark

mulling over all their conversations.
He remembered them down to the last 'er'.
There was so much he needed to get right.
He could never run out of stuff to add.

Music filled the room but missed him
and he'd fall asleep in the chair and dream

he was a city where everyone lived alone
in buildings that resembled smokers' lungs.

ECCENTRIC HAIR

There was something grinning on the telly:
Everything's creative, it said, meaning
staring at a shadow on the ceiling.
I didn't switch off, just sort of grunted.
I wasn't good for much at the time
except worrying about the first post
coming ten minutes after the second,
the cop who parked outside my house reading
How The CIA Murdered Bob Marley
and the gangsters who tailed me when
I went to the bank, to the shops, to the dentist.
I was low, listening to the same song
over and over: *Don't Tell Me You Don't Believe It*
& Call Yourself A Friend
and I'd no idea what I wanted,
other than to be able to relax
and see the funny side of things again,
maybe think back to being seventeen,
wishing I was Bob Dylan or someone
or at least had pretty eccentric hair.
I just needed to get out more, out of the house.

My suit was at the drycleaners so I wore jeans
and a denim jacket. I leaned against the bar
avoiding the eyes of the other customers:
the place was full of all the fools I'd ever been.
I heard them getting more and more maudlin.

LINGERIE ON A SOUTH YORKSHIRE CLOTHES LINE

1
Thirty-five years old and it was looking
like he'd always be a virgin. A woman once gave him

a short lift in her car
but it was a long time ago, they hadn't kept in touch.

Another time, stuck at a train station
in deep snow, just him and someone called Sue

huddled in front of an electric fire
in the waiting-room all night… maybe

she'd been married, he couldn't remember,
only the way her pale skin flushed.

Women were just pictures in magazines,
that was the way he tried to look at it.

He'd plenty of women, more than he knew what to do with.

2
Six pairs of knickers from next door's clothes line.
And a camisole top. He denied it

but the girl's brother thumped him anyway.
Well he was a weirdo, guilty or not.

His secrets included a pair of eyes
tattooed on his bell-end.

He'd been sixteen. The tattooist
who'd got him drunk and talked him into it

was arrested some years later, back of The Ship,
sucking off anyone who wanted it.

He'd put the tattooist out of his mind,
as much as was physically possible.

3
Eleven paperback novels,
including *Goldfinger*. And all the magazines

in heaps around the room,
torn-out pages sellotaped to the walls.

Bedclothes, unwashed for months.
A whip he'd used to thrash himself.

No mail. No address book
or note. No one to be informed.

A pint pot containing
nine pounds forty-nine pence in twos and ones.

III. DON'T WORRY

DON'T WORRY

A man in the Elephant and Castle
said there were games I should know more about,
I should try fags on the backs of my hands
or taking a shotgun to bed with me.
I recalled him dropped in the street one night,
the fine crack in his skull, the blood, the cold,
the copper who didn't think he'd make it.
'I tell thee lad, listen, what I don't know
about masturbation's not worth knowing.'
The place was suddenly brighter, I realised
I wasn't visible, he wasn't talking
to me at all. His brother came in then
with the news Clothes Line wouldn't be coming,
they'd been in a crash, all their fucking gear
was written off. A girl who followed them
from gig to gig began to shake her head.
'Don't worry' I told her, 'no one was hurt
except the bass player. His ribs showed through
his blood-soaked shirt as they tried to free him
from the snare drum.' I drank up and set off
along the canal, kicking at loose stones,
whistling one of the old songs I'm sick of,
sometimes stopping to see if I could spit
hard enough to reach the opposite bank.

UNTITLED, SOUTH YORKSHIRE, MID-EIGHTIES

1
When we get to The Wop
the barstaff are mopping up blood
and though it's only twenty past ten
the shits won't sell us a drink.
Except for a few hairies
clinging to pint glasses by the juke-box
the place is empty anyway.
It seems some smartarse in a suit
looked at one of the Angels
the wrong way, so they held him down
on the floor by the bar
(where the barstaff are now mopping)
and removed all his teeth—
'With a pair of pliers, and no
anaesthetic' says the landlord.
We talk him into selling us
a Guinness carry-out, he's not
too bad a bloke. Motorhead
have been in town, their fans
are all over the place
and on the train, grunting like apes.
One of them tosses off in the aisle,
looking up at the security camera
till someone else pulls it down
and starts a game of rugby with it.
Everyone is laughing.
A man with a glass eye
sits down next to me and tells me
I'm Nigel Fisher, child murderer

just out, and John turns round
and asks if he wants his eyes
to match. He looks
sort of startled, moves to another seat—
runs like a scalded bear
when he sees us getting off behind him
in Wombwell. Some miners
have overturned a police car
outside the Prince of Wales
and kicked the coppers unconscious.
Coppers are everywhere,
assaulting just about anybody.

2
Terry's drinking Newcastle Brown,
his right arm in plaster.
He's charged with threatening
behaviour and resisting arrest
but reckons the coppers haven't a case
and *he* ought to charge *them*.
After all, he says, he was only
fetching the paper and a bottle of milk.
We wonder about John, disappearing
without telling anyone anything.
Mr Barker weeps at the bar,
both his sons under arrest,
given terrible kickings.
People just ignore him.
The place is almost empty anyway.
Sam tells us about a snowman
built round a concrete post,
wearing a copper's helmet,

and some copper who drove fast
into it to flatten it
and is still on the sick, probably.
A woman with a broken arm
sits down at the next table with
a woman with a broken leg.
Sam's guilty of threatening behaviour.
Bound over, which prevents him picketing.
He's signed for the few hundred pounds
he'll pay back ten or twenty times
over the next four years, says
all the other people in the queue
wore bandages and plaster casts.
It was a big queue, one of the biggest.
A pale youth approaches, selling
SUN-FREE-ZONE stickers for the fund.

3

The off-licence and chippy
both go bust, it's a long walk
if you want anything now.
John writes from Bournemouth:
he's working in a health-food shop,
isn't coming back
till the strike's over
and the coppers gone.
George Barker shows everyone
his black and swollen balls.
His eyes seem to have grown wider,
taking over his face.
Two thousand coppers in armour
get one man into work at Cortonwood,

a convicted robber-with-violence.
A funny thing happens
on the way to Nottingham
only it's not really Nottingham
but Kettering and it's not really funny.
Be careful what you say,
the phones are tapped
and the man from *The Mail*
is looking for a good story,
that's him at the foot of the stairs.
Two coppers perjure themselves
but contradict each other
and Terry's found not guilty.
Fucking coppers, says a bearded man
from the Socialist Workers' Party
in a loud voice to nobody.
The place is almost empty.
If he's not a copper
then I'm Gabriele D'Annunzio.
Someone switches the telly on.
Oh aye, says Terry, who's that then?
Bob Geldof asks for donations:
the starving Africans, etc.

HYPHEN

The party was like the hyphen in Seymour-Smith.
The men were a stiff bunch, the women even worse.
I ended up pretending I'd the shits:
'Must have been the meat, I'm not used to it.'
We needed great mouthfuls of air, walked rather than
take a taxi. Jeanette took her shoes off
and her feet got dirty. She washed them in the sink
while I picked up a book. I read aloud,
it was pretty funny. You know the book I mean.
There was a lot of noise outside: dogs, screams
and Jeanette came and peered through the curtains,
leaving a trail of damp, talcumed footprints
which I pointed out when she turned back round.
'When are you going to get your clothes off?' she said.

ELSECAR RESERVOIR

Although languid on the surface
Elsecar reservoir is dangerous
to swim in. Underwater currents
can grab and drag you down
into a system of potholes.

I hear myself say this
and can hardly believe it.
Jeanette turns away, startled.
Old people are feeding ducks,
a few fishermen sit still.

Pike are another reason
for not swimming, I say.
They've been known to swallow
whole men, boys anyway,
let's put it like this—

It's looking like rain
says an old man with a cap
and a dog that cowers.
It weren't forecast though
he adds as he passes.

Let's put it like this,
you definitely wouldn't want
to go swimming with the fuckers.
I stop and sit on the bank,
feeling in my pocket for my fags.

One of the fishermen pulls in
a strange object, nothing
like a fish. Everyone
stands around discussing it
as it flip-flops on the bank

then suddenly it's down the bank and gone
before anyone can stop it.
Two girls aged four and six
start to cry in the next street.
We can hear them clearly

till the brass band starts up.
That's funny, Jeanette says,
I can hear a brass band
but I can't see it.
Seventy-Six Trombones is what they play

JEROME K. JEROME

Saying that *Three Men in a Boat*
was written by W. Somerset Maugham
drops my standing in The Milton
on a busy quiz night.

Two men and their shovels
are on the steps outside as I leave.
I remember them from the park.
One forces a fart as I pass.

REFUSED WATER

I said I'd paint the old couple's ceilings and walls
and now I am, in old clothes and with sheets
over the furniture. So much of it:
a double-bed, three armchairs, two sideboards, sofa.
You wouldn't think it's all that large a room either.

George keeps popping in to see how I'm getting on,
tells me all about himself, like the time
he walked it from Barnsley to Huddersfield,
it must have been 1927, he'd be eighteen.
He knocked on a door to ask for water

and was refused. He laughs at what he says
and I laugh too, perched like a Marx Brother
on top of the old, wobbly step-ladders.
Then a low shout from the next room
pulls his head round: Elsie, after the stroke.

George reckons she loves it, bossing him round:
build the fire up, do the washing and the shopping
and tidy up, make a cuppa, fetch the paper.
He never thought he'd end his days as a male nurse.
We've been married sixty-one years, he says.

I move the bed, uncover Elsie's loo.
George must have to help her on and off.
I push it back out of sight, get cracking.
He must wipe her, clean her, dispose of everything.
When the first coat's on I join them, say yes

please to a cuppa which I make myself.
The kettle takes an age to boil.
The kitchen is cold and dirty, too small.
I'll be old before long, with a kettle.
I hear Elsie asking George if it looks all right.

REMEMBERING DENNIS'S EYES

He always blinked too much,
like an overnight guest who leaves
with the toilet paper in his holdall
or leaves a dry blanket
covering a wet bed.
Even with the balaclava
turned round to hide his face
I could see him blinking
through the makeshift eyeholes.

Gimme the bastard bag
he yelled, tugging at it.
The iron bar bounced on
the guard's helmet five times
before he fell to his knees,
another four or five before
he lost his grip on the bag.
You saw nowt, *nowt*, Dennis hissed,
pinning me to the wall
with one hand, waving the bar
like a conductor with the other.

The last time I saw him,
years later, years ago,
he'd just tried to kill his ex-wife,
had been stopped by
his ten-year-old daughter.
He was running toward Darfield
like a wind-up toy
with a pair of kitchen scissors
sticking between his shoulder-blades.

TWO BOMBS ARE BETTER THAN ONE

for Martin Stannard

When I was younger I believe
that one day the Prime Minister
would have a slit

instead of a mouth,
tempting us to mail complaints
direct to his face.

I believed there'd be a just
and glorious war
every thirty minutes

and full employment
manufacturing arms
and legs for the wounded.

I thought everyone would know
the difference between
John Ashbery and John Ash

and a pile of sticks.
I thought people would care
about a pile of sticks.

I've heard it said
that when a man drops bombs
on soldiers, he's doing it

from the goodness of his heart.
I've heard it twice, not once.
Maybe it was more than twice.

IN PHIL'S BUTCHERS

They're sure they know me from somewhere:
'Aren't tha t' bloke that rode naked
on a bike through Jump for charity?
Thi picture wa' in t' Chronicle.'
The previous customer leaves, coughing
something red and green onto the pavement.
'That's a poorly mister, dead on ' is feet 'e is.'
One of them decides he worked
with my brother at Johnson's
though I've no brother who worked there.
'Are tha sure?' he wonders.
An older man (is it Phil?)
pops his head in from the back room:
'Leave t' lad alone 'n' gi' ' im ' is pies.'
I hold them in my hand as I say 'Ta-ra'
and leave, taking off my dark glasses.
There's a patch of blue sky
where my eyes should be, which startles
an old woman crossing the road.
'By' I say, to reassure her,
'it's cold enough for a walking stick.'
'All laughter is despair' she replies,
'it's t' human condition, like.'

THE NEXT MOVE
for Jim Burns

Think I'll write a story
about a nice young man
who through no fault of his own
becomes a werewolf.

Think I'll write a story
about someone who won't leave the house
on Friday the thirteenth
and gets electrocuted by their kettle.

Maybe one about someone
who won't leave the house
except on Friday the thirteenth
would be more interesting.

DEATH'S BOOTS
for Ian McMillan

In a previous incarnation, I climbed mountains
and sang my own praises, anticipating the trend.

On each wall of my home hung gaudy self-portraits.
I was posing for the camera before I invented it.

Then I was told I was a fool, that my career was over
for perfecting the ever-lasting light-bulb.

So I took a post kicking the oats out of farmers.
The money was good. Death's Boots, they called me.

I became involved because I saw no reason not to.
The reasons would pile up later like wood-shavings

from the pencils of the man who wrote *The American Century*.
That man was me, Death's Boots.

ETERNAL

Little nobodies
with big ideas
– don't think about them,
think about the woman
who'll be home soon,
who'll cross the room
in purple French knickers,
her navel deep enough
to slurp white wine out of.

Sheep, the (ha! ha!) eternal sentinels.

Outside, someone starts
strumming a guitar, badly.
The things people will do
to try to get applause.
You turn the radio on
to drown him out:
Everybody's dying
and some fool's singing about it.

Sheep, the (ha!) eternal (ha!) sentinels.

MEN WITHOUT CLOTHES
for my Mother

My mother says the young people across the yard
spend half their time running about naked.

They hold barbecues in the early hours
wearing nothing but glitter in their hair

and she has to tell them to be quiet
some people have to work for a living

and that they can't shock her: she used to be a nurse.
They look so daft, she says, men without clothes.

My father rustles the paper: How long will dinner be?
It'll be as long as it takes, my mother says.

THE ONLY SON AT THE FISH 'N' CHIP SHOP

He lived with his mother till he was forty-five
and no one was allowed to touch his head.

He worked on a novel for twenty years
without writing a word. He didn't like people

who wrote novels. He often drank. One glass of beer
was too many, two glasses weren't enough.

Travel brochures were as far as he went.
A football match, one time. He often said

Why would anyone want to think about a potato?
He painted his door with nobody's help.

THE VISIT

The only song he plays is 'What's in it for me?'
and I can't listen to it for too long

before I want a bucket to put over my head.
He asks how much I've made this year, how much

last year, how much I'll make over the coming year,
his voice sticking in my ears like an infection

nothing the doctor prescribes will clear up.
He has a pension plan, doesn't like me

spoiling his chance of getting value for money:
'You smoke too much' he says. And I do, in his house.

EXPERIENCE

He's glad of his experience
when he comes up against the likes of Sam.
He's bought her chocolates, tickets, flowers
and now, Christmas in mind, a pair

of expensive binoculars. He reckons
they're his best chance of winning her
before she turns forty. He loves her
record collection, similar to his own

only better, and she makes
a great chilli. He's learned
from past mistakes—you've got to give
women time to get used to the idea.

I wish him luck, as he lopes off
to the toilet, returning with
a packet of liquorice condoms
he waves across the table: 'Just in case.'

THE LAUGHING FACE

I think I've reached the age
where I become resigned
to certain things,
like my lack of interest
in almost everything
nearly everyone else
gets worked up about.
Like my own obsessions, this stuff
the least obscure of them.

I'd hate to be buried
while still breathing.
It could happen
without me noticing,
leave me with nothing
to look forward to
except the loss of consciousness.
It could have happened already,
or be happening right now.

Pretending things are fine
gets to be a habit.

Some people live longer
than they wanted
but never long enough.
They go deaf, have no one
to talk to, the lucky ones.

ENCOUNTER

The moment his mouth opened to say 'Hi'
was like a century of crass American heroes
and their effect on successive generations,
meatheads who cry into their beer at the drop of a coin,
the first incessant whine that comes along.
Maybe I should have screwed him up, put him in my pocket.
Instead, I bent over backwards not to stir up trouble.

Time passed slowly as he dragged me from pub to pub,
talking as if love had never been made,
which was also the way he walked. His tattooed lip
gave him the look of a thug not to be messed with,
it became unclear to me how we'd ever met.
I knew nothing about him, only that he was different
to any other psychopath I'd got drunk with;
for one thing, he was more likely to weep at odd times,
looking at me as if there was something
I could do or say to help, as if I would if I could.

SPOCK'S BRAIN

The best start to this year
would be to make a vow
and break it the minute
my head clears, something about
getting myself ship-shape,
sorted out. I'm not sure
if I'm drinking tea or
coffee or something else
but at least it's liquid.
When I pick up the paper,
I'm entitled to not
like what I see, or laugh
if there's anything funny
or not to laugh at.
I can raise my bushy
eyebrows all I want to,
make a face once or twice.
Sit here in my shirtsleeves
like a sane man who still
hopes things will get better.

Now I'm watching *Star Trek*,
an episode in which
Spock's brain is stolen,
leaving Kirk and the rest
less than forty minutes
before *Greece on a Tenner*
to search the galaxy,
find the brain and put it back
so Spock can say 'Thank you'
politely but coldly.

MEETING HUDSON

The holes in my teeth, and the broken bits,
can get to my concentration
at bad times. I'm ordering
at the beer festival, forget
and simply point, ending up with
Kelsall's Brainwhacker.
At the back of my head
I hear a woman say
'Mark's been busy with the new patio.'
I look round: Where is Hudson?
I've thirty pounds for him
burning a hole in my pocket.
I take my mind off it
with the great North Minnesota bank raid
of 1876. A few
liberties with the facts
were taken in *The Long Riders*.
I've cramp in both legs
but ignore it.

WHINING, CASCADING

You've spent days making tapes
so you can sell the records
for whatever you might get
which won't be much
but better than nothing.
Now your head's a compilation
of whining guitar solos
and cascading drum-breaks,
making it hard to think.
Not that you want to think.

The post. You've won
a cash prize. It could be
anything from five hundred
to sixty thousand pounds, or
it could be £1.
If you fill in the form
authorising your bank
to debit £9.75 a month
the cash prize will be sent to you.

Back from the supermarket
with some shopping, you find
a free wristwatch inside
the packet of tea-bags.
It occurs to you
you could buy the whole lot,
stock up with enough tea
to last a couple of years,
then stand on a corner

and sell the watches.
But you don't have enough
capital to cover
the original investment.

PRAYING FOR A MIRACLE

I'm walking down Cherry Tree Street
in the early afternoon
of my fourth day without a smoke.
The wet roofs seem wrongly-set
to the houses, as if they might
slide off at any moment.
A landscape shaped by subsidence
where a man in a leather jacket
uses a small cup to bail rainwater
from a purple fibre-glass topless beach-buggy.
Hey, he shouts, cigarette smoke
all over him, don't I know thee?
I think not, I cross the road, I go in
an off-licence and stand behind
two girls spending twenty pence
on a variety of small sweets,
taking their time, changing their minds
then changing them back, making
the fat young man behind the counter
sigh. He wants to watch the snooker
on the small black-and-white TV
in the doorway behind him.
He has a stool there to sit on,
and an open can of beer
and smoking cigarette on a shelf,
and I turn round and walk out
without buying cigarettes or anything.
The beach-buggy has a nameplate:
Helter Skelter. On the side.
I'm an hour or hour and half

from the place where I can shake
the money-tin, rattle the coins.
It'll sound good, like more.
It'll sound like wealth, enough
to start a new life with.

NOT CALIFORNIA

Time passes slowly here in South Yorkshire.
The dustbin men came yesterday. Maybe
it was the day before, the day the couple
passed the house and had this conversation:
'What do you mean, I'm the one that's to blame?'
'You're the one that's to blame, that's what I mean.'
They said this three times, then they were out of
my life for ever.

Something I've never done is fly a hang glider.
I'm embarrassed about so many things.
I'm lazy, a weakling, can't even stop smoking.
My cough gets on my nerves but at least I own it.

So much for the jolly version.
On this binge I'm flat on my back
on the living-room floor, too smashed
to unlock the door for my wife.
She's shouting my name, banging the window,
looking at me as if to say
It's three in the afternoon, for God's sake
what are you up to?

She's back at ten. I'm still flat out of course, and wake
slowly, unsure where I am, hearing the tapping
at the window without understanding.

This is a small room. It's true it could be smaller.

HALF DEAF

If I'd never listened to music on headphones
and drank all night, I'd be a different person,
either the village idiot
or the most desperate man you'd ever set eyes on.

With Nothing But A Brick Wall To Look At (And My Eyes Shut),
that's the name of that song. I could have got well drunk
in the time it's taken to remember.
All I had to go on was the harmonica solo.

I only hear half of what I believe.
I understand it could be like this for some time.
I need a holiday, have to settle
for pinning postcards to the walls instead.

SWAMP MUSIC

The band are starting up in the corner.
They're called Swamp Music: two lead guitarists,
a lot of hair. The vocalist
looks like he did three years on a chain gang
or do I only want to believe that?
He can't sing but the band are as good as they get

for Barnsley—I'm grinning, can't stop.
This is the place someone threw a pint glass,
missing Terry's head by inches, denting the wall
so deep I'm sure it would have been fatal.
I wasn't there, but saw the dent later.
Terry showed me, wide-eyed with something like wonder.

RECKLESS

I called to make contact
with someone still living, he says.
You're just hungover, I tell him,
pull yourself together.
No, he says, I've passed out
at too many parties.

Now we're off to a football match.
He always drives too fast. We cross the line
and head straight at a transit van,
Lynyrd Skynyrd on the cassette,
sounding muted
with just one speaker working.

SOMETHING UNFIXED

There's nothing insulting
about the rain,
it's everybody else
owning cars
makes me feel insulted,
walking back from the shops
with plastic bags
cutting into my fingers
and my shoes leaking.
Today's insults
already include
hearing that homelessness
isn't a tragedy,
merely unhappiness,
and it's not even ten a.m.
I pass a man who wishes
he could afford to go
to the dentist, another
whose wife is deteriorating.

THE PERSUADERS

A well-known nobody
is opening The Countryman in Wombwell
and some people are ridiculous enough
to turn up and ask for his autograph.
He's ridiculous enough to sign them.
Twenty years on, we sit arguing

over who it was: Tony Curtis? Or
Roger Moore, before he was James Bond?
The beer's warm and a rockabilly band
are trying to pretend electricity
hasn't been invented. The harmonies are great
if you like that kind of thing. When we leave

the six of us walk in single file
up the narrow street that takes us
past The Angler's Rest and The Ship
and the Conservative and Catholic clubs
and British Legion and Royal Oak
and The Alma and Little George
and into the Horse Shoe,
where the barmaid is a comedienne:
'Good evening, ladies and beasts.'
It's Nev's round.

On the Buses with Dostoyevsky

Bloodaxe, 1994

I

THE NEW MR BARNSLEY SOMETHING

on the front page of the *Chronicle*
once promised to crack my skull
but that's beer down the urinal

and I can turn to page two
as calmly and as amused
by his pectorals as anyone else

recalling also one Saturday night
as part of a large crowd watching
Mr Barnsley Something bouncing

another man's head on a car bonnet
while shouting 'I'll teach thee
to make eyes at our lass.'

And suddenly I wonder
what became of him—
the other man,

the one they lifted
like a ticking bomb
and drove away, slowly.

SCARED

She's scared of wanting books
in tidy piles, of making sure
everything's in its proper place;

she's sure the same desire
was behind the skyscraper
supplanting the teepee

and is why maps on walls
have flags sticking in them
which uniformed men discuss.

Most days she goes nowhere,
just sort of potters round
trying not to notice

everything out of place.
She listens to the great masters,
she can talk to the cat

or hit the gin and write
letters to her only sister
who died some years ago.

STOP

'I have to spend the rest of my life with this fool,'
the woman said, jabbing her thumb at a man

wearing stained overalls and carrying
a welding helmet. I took no notice,

hoped the bus would come soon. I was on my way home
after some months of clandestine research

in the sort of place criminals would plan
a necessary assassination.

'I'm stuck with it now, God I'm stuck with it alright,
stuck with it whether I want him or don't.'

People went in and out of the bank opposite.
I felt stupid looking at them, looked at the ground.

I knew what to expect when I made my report.
I was naming names, they wouldn't like it.

What they liked wasn't my concern, but what they'd do.
They'd had things their own way for a long time.

All of a sudden I realised
I was facing downhill and not uphill.

The bus came and the couple made no move.
The man spoke for the first time: 'We don't want this one.'

It meant I was at the front of the queue, in fact
was the queue. I made it to the back seat, slid down

as far as I could, my knees high
on the back of the seat in front. I thought

of Robert Ford taking the time to aim
and a hundred other sneaky bastards

and didn't even breathe. The man threw the helmet
at the woman's feet as the bus pulled out.

NERVOUS BEFORE BREAKFAST

A leafless tree, catprints in snow
And he doesn't notice, stone-faced always

Spraying anti-freeze all over his car
Every morning, as he gets in it, an alarm blares

You crush whatever's in your hand
You're beginning to think and act like him yourself

Leaving rubbish where you know it'll annoy him
Slamming doors at half-five in the morning

Raised voices, breaking glass, a normal day

'In our experience, the murderer
is often the last person to see the victim alive'

You turn the radio off. There's nothing else to turn on

A HUGE BAG OF POTATOES

A huge bag of potatoes
is carried home by a woman
past a row of houses
where men are swearing
as they take the football results
from the BBC teleprinter.
The woman holds the bag
close to her body with both arms.
She's tired, looking forward
to sprucing up in a cool bathroom.

The sun's in now, but earlier
the men sat supping pints
on the steps of the Clothier's Arms,
down to their vests or bare-chested;
men with muscular arms
and beer-bellies, tattoos
and reddening flesh, moustaches
and stubble. The woman
passed them then, and they
stared after her backside.

Now she reaches her house
and puts the bag down
 feels in her pocket.
As she produces her keys, the door
opens, and a muscular, tattooed arm
picks up the bag
like a rabbit by the ears
and takes it inside.
The woman follows
and the door closes.

POEM FOR BILLY

His wife's thrown him out
again, this time
for going to Cleethorpes
for the weekend. He'd gone

Friday, instead of work—
meant to get back
early evening, ended up
too drunk. He'd phoned

to say he was still at work,
the car wouldn't start
and it might take a while
to get it fixed, it looked like a—

'What's that noise?' she'd said.
'What noise Luv?' 'Tha knows
what fuckin' noise,' she'd said,
'them fuckin' seagulls bastard.'

He opens another can of John Smith's.
'So ah stayed till Sunday neet.
Might us well gerrung
fer nickin' a sheep us a tha knows what.'

WOMAN'S TEA PARTY

He comes in with his tray
and black armband,
injects himself in the eye,
starts whistling
'They Smoked My Cigars
But Were Good Enough
to Leave the Ash',
then hangs upside-down
from the light-fitting
and pours out the cups
 snarling the whole time.
Tiny headless animals
fall from his pockets,
also, a bag of
blood-stained broken glass.
When he's finished,
he sorts out a few bones
that he gnaws in the corner,
sitting on his heels.

MEANINGLESS INCIDENT

He slumps down
in the seat next to us,

blood dripping
from a large gash

near the knuckles
of his right hand,

staining his jeans.
He wraps a cloth

round the wound,
picks up his pint,

smiles at Jeanette
as he takes

one of my cigarettes,
asks if I'd like

a game of pool.
The word LEGEND

in purple ink
on his forehead.

BUILDER

One day he'll get the help
he needs—till then
we'll just have to put up
with him, marching
up and down the street
with his tape measures,
hammer and saw, lumps of wood.
Last week he built a fence
all round Mrs Barton's—
we could just make out
the top of her head,
hear her frail cries…

'Mornin' ter yer,'
he says to me;
he's knocking a steel post
into my front doorstep;
'nearly done, nearly done'.

BOSSES

Every morning
I open the back door
to get a chestful
of fresh air, the cat
strolls in
and I feed it. Today
someone's freezing
up a telegraph pole,
a group of bosses
smirking at the foot,
discussing the next step.
I stand in the doorway
while the kettle boils
in this run-down
South Yorkshire pit village
that has no pit,
that has no theatre,
that has no crowds of tourists
photographing gardens,
that has no path leading
to a bookshop. I stand
and listen to the bosses talk.

ON THE BUSES WITH DOSTOYEVSKY

Because of the steelworks
that deafened my dad
our telly was always
too loud, so loud
it formed a second narrative
to what I was reading
up in my room
in my late teens—I'd have
Hemingway and *Kojak*,
Alias Smith and Jones and Poe.
All that noise! Car chases
and gunshots, sirens, screams,
horse racing and boxing,
adverts for fish fingers,
floor cleaner and fresh breath;
and Knut Hamsun starving,
Ahab chasing his whale.
I felt like a learner driver
stalled at a traffic light,
a line of lorries behind me.
Because of the steelworks
that closed in 1970
and which I never saw
except as a skeleton,
I like silence and calm,
I like silence and smoke
cigarettes in the dark.

ACQUAINTANCE

He's turned bitter and serious,
the fear of death
muddling up his conversation.

It's no laughing matter.
It's as if irony
was just something he grew out of.
He can't look forward
to a death bed,
has no famous last words.

He annoys me, I don't like him
sitting across from me
while I'm eating biscuits.
I don't like him
telling my jokes, claiming they're his,
expecting me to laugh.

I could pass the biscuits
and he wouldn't thank me.
I could choke and he wouldn't move.

BRAVO

They've got a cheap mortgage
on a two bedroom end terrace
and have stolen some land
adjoining the property
to make a drive
for their silver Bravo.
They're building a dream home,
it's the only thing they're able
to talk about.
They go in carrying pieces,
are trying hard.
They've never stopped,
and their youthful faces
can't hide the mounting excitement—
before too long they'll be ready
to sell, buy
that three bedroom semi-detached
on the street where no one will think
anything different to them.
They're keen to get away
from ruffians
who play music too loud,
too loud being at all.

'It's dead simple,' says Mark,
'I'm phoning the police.'
'Yes Mark,' says Jean, 'phone them.'
Mark phones the police; the police
laugh their socks off
when they get there.

GRACE

died in a hospital bed
surrounded by her family.
She'd been unconscious
days on end
then suddenly sat up and
looked her husband
right in the eye.
They were both
eighty-three.

I sat there
a while, just her and me.
I wanted to believe
somehow, somewhere, something
of her still lived.
I held her hand
and thought about a dream
I'd had when I was four.
Grace saved me from a lion,
beating it off with a poker
at the top of the cellar steps.

NUMBERED

Dirty buses, always crowded.
The sign above the shop says FLOREST.
Bottles and chip papers
piling up at the curb, a young girl
with the blankest face
pushing a beat-up pram—
I'd take off if I could,
just leap into the air
and glide away over the church steeple.

Last night a distressing experience.
While crunching toast
a lower back tooth broke in half.
It doesn't hurt but it doesn't seem right
not to do anything about it.

I tell someone at the workshop
that the days of the community newspaper
are numbered.
The days of the community
are numbered, he replies.

High on my list of necessities
is a warm room where I can hear
the sound of people going places,
the clacking of high heels
as I trawl through old books and pamphlets
for the one true classic
I've forgotten all about
that will bring joy into my life.

HER PLACE

Her fridge wasn't working
and a bucket of water
in the corner of her room
was stuffed with bottles of lager
and cheap white wine
while she danced with her eyes closed
in this bent-kneed way she had
to the jazz station
her radio stayed tuned in to.
I stood in the doorway
grinning, with a cigarette,
not sure if she knew I was there or not.
Then she smelled the smoke,
opened her eyes and saw me.

She'd attempted suicide
half a dozen times
and complained constantly
of headache, toothache, backache,
and that she needed a man.
She walked with a theatrical limp.
'Darling,' she'd say, 'I am in such pain today.'
Everyone was 'Darling',
male or female,
and she was always in pain.
I used to go to her place once a month
to buy tobacco.
She knew a lorry driver
and sold it cheap.

DATE

He checks his hair
in the mirror
and his teeth
being a cause for concern
rehearses
a different smile.

His wife lives on
in his parrot
squawking
Put that guitar down
till you bloody
learn to play it.

II VOLUNTEER

For Joe and Jaffa Dana

HOLY AIR

I

This is where Jesus gave his life.
It's illegal to drive a bus unarmed
and the drivers wear side-holsters,
strut round the station like a posse.
A dozen soldiers share the seats with you,
nursing their rifles, never letting go.

This is where Jesus gave his life
and the bazaars are full of it.
You need money, a lot,
and Arabs will follow you down the street—
'I can sell you a jar of Holy Air
at a reasonable price.'

II

'This street is closed,'
says a young Arab boy
suddenly blocking my path,
'bad Muslims.'
He holds out his hand
and I give him a shekel
as the call to prayer
rolls across the rooftops.
God is great! he shouted
as he detonated the bomb
strapped to his chest.
Something like this happens
and does not stop.

NOT FOR AESTHETIC

I'm to work with Mario,
an Argentinian carpenter
who's been on the kibbutz
six years. He arrives
on a bicycle, a white Labrador
trailing behind. With winter
peeping round the corner,
it's important we paint
the outside of some new
wooden buildings. 'Not
for aesthetic, but to…'
He blinks behind his glasses
and waves his hands,
his English failing him.
'Protect,' I say.
'Yes,' he says.
Today though the sun is hot
and I take off my shirt,
can feel my back roasting
as I slap grey paint
unceremoniously.
It's hard to believe
it's November; back home
they'll be buttoning big coats,
wrapping their scarves.
But Mario insists
that here too it will be cold
and raining before long.
He constantly apologises
for his English:

'I study it five years
two hours each week
but I never speak it.'
Really I have no trouble
understanding him, though
he doesn't seem to get
much of what *I* say.
'It's my northern accent,'
I tell him, 'we're poor
and can't speak properly.'
'In Argentina, the south
poor and the north…'
'Prosperous.'
'Yes.' And later,
the work done, walking home,
Mario pushing his bicycle
and the dog trotting
alongside, nosing the grass
for lizards or hedgehogs,
I try to tell him more
about the north of England—
the pits shut, the unemployment,
Thatcher's legacy.
'In my country,' he says,
'we call the Malvinas
Thatcher's war.'
The dog runs barking
to the foot of a tree.
'In mine too,' I reply
in my clearest English.
He nods, and shouts something
at the now frantic dog.

NOVEMBER

The young Israelis
accept their lot.
Here at this kibbutz breakfast table
are a dozen, boys and girls
who'll soon be soldiers.
And the long hair of the boys,
hanging over the backs
of their Jim Morrison
and Nirvana t-shirts,
or tied in ponytails,
and the rings through the noses
of the girls and some boys,
will go, must go, in March.
November, they sit
cheerfully eating eggs
and reading their newspapers
back to front, left to right:
five soldiers wounded slightly
near the Lebanese border;
one killed in a drive-by shooting
in the quiet town of Safad;
three killed, one left paralysed
by a suicide bomber
at Netzarim junction.
This is the daily news.
And I sit with them
and chew toast and jam,
thirty-eight and British
and safe, and wonder if
any will make the news
themselves?

VOLUNTEER

You're not sure if it's Monday or Wednesday—
you're working eight hours a day, six days a week;
you don't have a television
or anything happening socially
to distinguish the days.
You can forget who you are,
what you are, back home, all that.
You've done your shift in the kitchen;
your shoes are split from standing in water;
now you cherish the hot earth
beneath your bare feet
as you sit nursing a beer
while your skin darkens.
You can pick up the *Jerusalem Post*,
squinting in the sun as you read
'the rabbi was shot several times in the head and face and lost
        control of his car.'
You can put it back down.
You can play backgammon
with a South African who says
'Do you mind if I'm white? I wouldn't want to be black.'
Which makes it a pleasure
to beat him.

PIPER

At the age of thirty-seven
he owns only what he stands in
and enough stuff to fill a duffel bag
but he's not worried.
He stopped worrying about the future
the day he left Germany
to avoid the draft,
losing himself in Amsterdam
with a woman who could keep up.
He made a living.
The day the police arrested him
he had a ticket to see Dylan—
for more than one decade
this had been an ambition.
Instead, he got to spend two years
reading Albert Camus and Herman Hesse,
Charles Bukowski and Jack Kerouac.
It was like being back
in the orphanage.

Pale and skinny, hardly
a word to say for himself.
We see him quickly change
into a muscular, tanned raconteur,
holding court on his porch
all afternoon and evening
until something, the past
or some version of the future,

puts a bottle of vodka
firmly in his hand
and clouds his eyes.
And he's turning up for work drunk,
seven in the morning.

TOWN

There's always a saxophone
in the background of a scene like this
or at least a trumpet.
Which doesn't make it any less real,
but as you approach the building
you're hearing a soundtrack
that exists only in your head.
Rain gathers in large holes,
making you hop along the pavement,
while taxi-drivers give rough rides,
leaning over the back seat saying
'They ought to get off their butts.'
You can't go in a lot of these places
without being questioned briefly,
perhaps searched for guns or explosives.
But the saxophone helps you through it
though there are no saxophones here.

A WEEK

They pose for photos
with leggy blondes, the young soldiers,
will even let them stroke their rifles—
this within a hundred metres
of the Wailing Wall,
where the black-suited, bobbing hassidim
chant their prayers.
Only because of the soldiers
are the hassidim safe,
and the soldiers detest them—
frisk them brusquely at checkpoints,
then shove them on with a sneer
and leave the likes of me unmolested.

A week in Jerusalem
is like the rest of your life.
Each morning in the café
just inside Jaffa Gate
I'd see the same European
sitting by the window,
already on his third or fourth beer,
rubbing bloodshot eyes
as the sun struck the silverware,
now and then jotting something
in a small notebook,
afterwards shutting it sharply
with an aggrieved sigh.

BOTH LIARS

They were both liars, boring as well,
though the girl falling out of the window
story was at least
energetic. The eldest
was drunk, an idiot half the time,
unconscious the rest.
'You don't like to talk to me,' he said,
vodka in my face in a bus
on the way to the Dead Sea.
'No, I like to,' I replied,
'but not at six in the morning.'
That evening I'd see him
throw a mattress round a garden
furiously, shouting
in his own language.
I'd stand and watch
for a quarter of an hour.

The young one was different,
walked in on us making love,
stood in the doorway
not three feet from the bed
and talked about a phone call
he was expecting.
Simple was not the word.
He pummelled a punchbag
suspended from a tree
for one hour each afternoon
beneath a scorching sun.
And he'd run, for one hour,

then sit staring into space
while he got his breath back
for two hours.
The day they escorted the drunk one
onto the bus, making it clear
he'd better not come back,
the punchbag one forgot
to punch his bag.
Then remembered.

SOMETHING FROM A STUPOR

He held a bottle of Gold Star up
and peered into it solemnly.
Told me for the tenth time
he was just 'one of the guys',
something reptilian
about the stare he fixed me with
through the green glass of the bottle.
He was young enough to be a son
I'd disown,
the sort of man who'd rip
somebody's photo to pieces.
He glanced from face
to face, grinning;
the two fat blokes at our table
left with their expensive cameras.
'We don't need them,' he said, and
laughed, 'I don't need anybody.'
Then the noise started, the disco,
and he was off and dancing,
leaving behind his untouched beer
and a smell like gunpowder.
I saw him only one more time, a glimpse,
just before the place closed
at five in the morning,
of a small group of men his own age
herding him through the door,
his cries
drowned out
by *Trenchtown Rock*.

THE CHICKENS

Like a spiv
from the Second World War
he passes the chickens
through the dishwasher hatch,
turns and gets away quick
as I stuff them
in my laundry bag.

Two more hours
and the shift will be done.
I'll be in the shower,
then playing backgammon
in the afternoon sun.
The chickens defrosting.
None of us

can stomach
another kibbutz dinner—
cottage cheese, green peppers,
boiled eggs, stale bread.
The chickens down to me,
I'll sit back while the rest
do the work.

Tapping my feet
to the rhythm guitar.
The fire in the darkness,
our shapes huddled round it.
The meat sizzling, spitting.
The dogs inching closer,
told to lie down.

MASSACRE

I'm on my morning break,
trying to eat corn flakes
while taking the news in.
Everyone's stunned by this one:
Suicide bomber, Beit Lid junction.
Twenty-two soldiers killed,
all aged eighteen, nineteen, twenty.

Henri has the day off.
His long hair tucked under a hat,
he sits with his cigarettes
and coffee, waiting for a lift
to a school reunion
at a graveside in the city.
No one wants to talk

or risk meeting someone
who hasn't heard.
All round the room
people push their plates aside,
the food only picked at.
They go back to work early,
each with the same stooped gait.

The *Jerusalem Post* has photos
of all those who died.
They crowd pages two and three
with youthful smiles,
with eyes that do not blink,
that gaze confidently
at the future.

DISHWASHER

She turns the radio
louder and lights
one of my cigarettes.
She's seventeen
and sick to death of what
we have to do.

Down on my hands and knees
scrubbing the drains
I stare at her bare feet
as she dances.
They're so brown and pretty
I almost faint.

Later, our chief tells her
she doesn't care
about her work.
'It's bad enough,' she says,
'to have to *do* this job,
do I have to care too?'

BRUISE

Since I slipped
and spent fifteen minutes
on my back moaning
at the hub of a circle
of concerned and amused faces
I've had pins and needles
in my right hand. I thought
I'd broken my elbow
but it was only bruised.
The doctor gave me some painkillers
which have a real buzz,
better than the vodka – 'wodka'
it says on the bottles here.
Actually, the wodka
tastes like petrol, not that

I've ever drunk petrol.
Listen, a few minutes ago
I put down Norman's book.
It was archetypal Norman,
I mean he was just
blowing his own trumpet,
and he doesn't even have
a very good one—
he must have bought it
at Woolworth's
back in the seventies.
'What was the book like?' Jeanette asks.
'It was interesting,' I reply,
'as was having a toe amputated
when I was nineteen.'

PIPER AGAIN

He comes out at ten,
joins me on the porch.
The morning's hot;
we're in our shorts,
bare-chested, barefoot.
He can't remember
much of what happened—
he walked home about five,
the sun was coming up.
I watch his tattoos jerking
as he coughs, clutching his ribs.
Did I still have that bottle of wine,
did I think I could get it for him?
'I need it very quickly.'
By twelve it's finished
and I'm on my way to lunch;
he's not hungry,
and has managed
to get hold of
six bottles of beer.
'Bon appetit!'
he shouts after me,
over the radio.

EYAD'S CASSETTE TAPE

The night before we leave
Eyad arrives from Qalqilya
to shake hands and say goodbye
and give us a cassette tape—
'good Arab music, something
to remember me with.'
I'm too drunk to talk properly
to a man who never drinks
but he's used to it
and knows I'm being stupid
when I ask if he'd like
a game of chess; he only
taught me the rules a month ago.
Eyad, who was surprised
to hear there was poverty
and despair in England too.

The afternoon at Ben Gurion
is sweaty, two security women
grilling us for thirty minutes already
when one asks if anyone
gave us anything to put in our bags?
Even as I say no
I remember the cassette tape
and just for an instant
Eyad is not a friendly,
intelligent and humane person
but just another young Muslim
who wants to kill Jews
to be sure of a place in Heaven

but whatever I think
it seems my face stays the same
because the security women
don't doubt I'm not carrying
anything suspicious.

THE BARKING OF STRAY DOGS

The barking of stray dogs
outside my window
in the middle of the night
doesn't bother me
any more, not a bit,
well maybe a bit.
So much is funny
it's hard to know where to finish—
behaving like one
of the Blues Brothers,
or spending the whole day
slicing carrots, a man of my
whatever.

Tequila is good
mixed with grapefruit,
if you've the patience
to squeeze them. Traffic passes
and is not noticed,
like the early stages
of a mental illness.
The locals' word for a hangover
is also their word
for a stray dog.

POLITICS

It's like watching a film
of your own funeral.
You're shouting I'M ALIVE
but no one can hear you.

Across a room, two men
assess each other's silence.
They yawn and cough,
cross and uncross thin legs.

It takes years.
Ice forms on the cameras
that bring us news.
And then the men nod,

and then they rise.
One claps, then holds up a hoop
the other leaps through.
They both shout BOOM!

HOME VIDEO

Everything's still in boxes, and Jeanette
eats a boiled egg out of the centre of a toilet roll.
'Maybe we could make these for a living?' I say,
'there's always plenty of fools, they'll be queuing up

to buy toilet roll egg cups.' She dips a soldier,
I switch the radio on. I can't say what it is
but I wouldn't call it music. The tuner sticks
at the station, I can't move it… At least

the phone's connected; it rings; 'Hello?'
'It's about time I gave you a piece of my mind,'
says Norman. 'Don't make it too big a piece,'
I reply, 'or you won't have any left.'

MANUSCRIPT DISCOVERED BEHIND A BATHROOM TILE

I can't play guitar any more,
my fingers have got soft.
I never *could* play, but
at least I used to try.
The neighbours, true to form,
didn't like it one bit.
'If people want to live
next door to a churchmouse,'
I used to say, 'they should
move into a churchyard.'

Back then, I loved cats, loved
to have them around me.
There were ten or fourteen of them,
the only things
I didn't want to hurt.
They'd go to sleep with me, purring.
I used to imagine
drinking myself to death
and ending up half-eaten
before I was discovered.

It's true I was drinking,
working on a novel:
CONVERSATIONS WITH DISGUSTING LITTLE GEEZERS.
It was all written just like
that in upper case.
I'd get up, type a few pages,
get drunk, try to play my guitar.
Then I'd be ready to go back to bed.

I remember the day
I made a pile of the pages
and quietly tore them;
it was winter, quite cold;
I'd had a dream the night before
that I lived in a town
where *Little House on the Prairie*
was what life was actually like.
I knew at that moment
I couldn't have a novel inside me,

that all my attempts to get serious
would always end with a chuckle.
These days I try to keep my life simple,
but sooner or later
I'm left with no choice but
to seek out a clean shirt.
If I remember to comb my hair,
I comb it. I shake my head
as I read the morning paper,
which makes my life worthwhile.

POEM MENTIONING A SWEEPING BRUSH

It was the ugliest room of the lot.
Well, they expected him to live in it.
Of course he said he'd take it, and the job,
being badly in need of a good meal.

Six months (half a year!) he did it, learning
to use a sweeping brush the proper way,
leaning on it when no one was watching.

Sometimes he'd count the change in his pocket
and try to imagine where he'd end up.
It had taken the best part of his life
to realise that not everyone

had always been wrong. Now everything
was as clear as the skin on a snare drum,
as an army marching across his tongue.

STILL GRINNING

The black boys on the train, three of them, in high spirits
are darting up and down the aisle,
whacking each other over the head
with rolled-up copies of discarded
Independents and *Guardians*,
their laughter filling the carriage
like a soundtrack from a shoestring movie,
and the other passengers, white mostly, over sixty,
the corners of their mouths turned down
in the way of religious fanatics
who've stumbled across a peep-show,
are looking at them like they could kill them
or put them in a cage for the rest of their lives—
the black boys oblivious
or else knowing but not giving a shit.
Their noise makes me grin for the whole journey,
till I get off at the place I've moved to,
where almost all the old whites get off too,
to board the bus that takes them into town,
that passes me when I'm halfway up the hill,
panting and still grinning.

SIX WAYS TO SAY O.K.

Church clock announcing midnight like a patriarch
It's been time to go to bed for centuries

Drunk shoes, drunk suit and tie, drunk cigarette
Eyes like a horse with its guts hanging out

Drunk key, drunk door and doormat, drunk light-switch
Drunk armchair beckoning

*

The evening was a joke I'd heard before
I swallowed something that left a bad taste

It was friendship or acted quite like it
Had to pull his fingers out of my throat

Two-faced liar harbouring a grievance
He borrowed my moustache permanently

*

My head is a vandalised slot machine
I look out from it like a hanging judge

The trick is to pretend the noise has stopped
It's not always easy

A paper boat for a paper journey
See the bloated corpses in the blue pool

*

When I look at the clock I see faces
A man with a too-pretty wife sat weeping

They put the best traps where you least expect
Who the hell is 'They'? They is them and them

The breath in a party balloon knows this
A cigar knows it, and a bloody war

*

Sometimes you speak and no one takes notice
Or they mishear, call you John when you're Bob

You wipe your sweating brow on a towel
You look in the mirror: you know that guy

Sometimes you have to stand on the table
You have to shout. You have to shout louder

*

I can see the clock and what time it is
A young woman accepts a cigarette

Something worth looking at, and then the drums
I said let's go, why not? I said, let's go

Making love the couple were astonished
The loudness of midnight, then the laughter

GOD AND BANANAS

In the letter he complained of tiredness.
He was tired, he wrote, of losing at chess
and winning at chess, tired of being drunk
and not being drunk, tired of drunks talking
about god and bananas, egg-timers
and elephants. He was tired of wishing
he'd said something, then saying it; he said
he was tired most of all of being tired.

He knows this is the room where he will die,
leaving nothing to remember him by
but a brown stain on the ceiling above his bed.
He re-reads the letter about tiredness,
like someone searching for something precious
on their hands and knees and almost sobbing.

STRAIGHT

I can't trust anyone
who doesn't doubt himself some of the time.
I can always hear him,
like a radio that can't be switched off
coming through a thin wall.
I had friends but they disappeared
like smoke through an open window.
I keep ticking over, I don't know how
in this drab place
where everything gets taken for granted.
I stare at the damp patch on the ceiling,
at the hole worn in the carpet.
I say 'hello' on my doorstep
in the sun, it's not hard.
I spray weeds on the path, whistling
in an old pair of jeans.

JUPITER

I've been lost in a study of Jupiter.
Thirty-three hundred times the size of earth

but no movie industry to speak of,
hence no awards ceremonies and no

microphones in the faces of nothing.
I explained all this in the town centre

but people seemed eager to ignore me.
Ah, people. They like to think they know me

by my black moustache and curly red wig
and the wheelchair I push in front of me

containing the rag doll, ukulele,
and ghetto blaster I sing along with.

They know my favourite song is *Love Me Do*,
which I croon to a punk backing, they know

my coat for all weathers is grey cotton.
They don't know how I ache in these old bones.

They know yobbos sometimes gang up on me.
They don't know what the boots taste like.

HOW IT WENT

I

'O.K., let's do it. It won't be the first time
I've travelled in a car boot…'

He seems to be sleeping
less and less, up at four, washed and shaved
and wide awake by five – on good mornings
he feels like the first goat
able to play piano with its teeth.

The news is a series of pranks,
a schoolboyish humour he must have grown out of.

Returned from a severe haircut
and with nothing in his pocket
he smokes a cigarette that hits his chest
like a hammer. And stares through the window
at the departing summer.

II

He is a sap, he knows this for a fact,
evidence is all around him
like silly wallpaper, a bookcase full of books
he's never read, never will read.
But people traipsing round the streets
with briefcases and narrow minds?
He'd nail his tongue to the back door
rather than take part in all that.
Hungry, he opens a tin of mushy peas,
eating them cold, with a teaspoon, in the darkness.

III

He can't believe for one minute
that a man could transform
into a bird by force of will.
A pig, maybe, but not a bird, no way.
It's hard to imagine anything
less like a man than a bird—
or, come to think of it, a pig,
a friendly creature
that wishes no one harm,
content to live out its time
with its face in a trough
without ever seeking to explain it
or look beyond it.
They're the last things a man could end up as,
however hard he tried.
No amount of practice would help.

IV

He holds the newspaper up, shaking it.
'Have you heard about this?' he asks.
He replies that he hasn't, so he tells
himself all about it for the third time.

He opens the window to let some air in, some noise.
'Someone who notices nothing
suddenly notices something!'
he shouts at the astonished passers-by.

THE VISIT

He came over about three months ago.
He got drunk. I got drunk. My wife got drunk.
Then we put him on a train and went to bed.

He'd blathered on about so many things—
his wife, his son, his teeth, his dog, prison.
I remember it like a burning hand.

He said he wished he'd been alive
before science and mass entertainment,
before all the magic became debunked,

and knew for a fact we were all equally doomed.
He had the evidence. I sighed
when he started to produce it—

box after box, cutting after cutting
covering twenty years, twenty damn years
of downright bloody single-mindedness.

RUM AND BLUE SKY

It was the time of day he liked the most,
before everyone got busy.
Just the one drink, straight down, then he was out,
striding along the disused railway track,
his old dog barely able to keep up.
All those people! He had no time for them,
them or their dull regulations.
He'd had no choice in jail, they'd seen to that;
that was part of it. Well he was free now.
He reached the bridge where he always turned back;
the sky was a clear blue pressed handkerchief.
He felt the weight of the bottle, kissed it,
took a mouthful of rum and kept going.

Through it all he'd stayed true to his own dreams.
And here he was, breathing. Even his dog
seemed to hear the promise the day whispered
to soar like a frisbee thrown at the sun.
He adjusted the cardboard in his shoes.
He was humming something joyful, something
he couldn't put a name to but knew well.

THE ANKLES

The ankles of the woman
and the red open-toed sandals

on the stone steps as she descends
from the insurance offices—

and my head had been brimming
over with money problems!

The street full of summer,
fresh air slapping my face

like a woman trying to wake me up—
those aches in my joints, I'll ignore

them, and now
two young girls who might be sisters

cross the road with a pushchair,
their faces shining with laughter.

ABOUT SOMETHING

The life and soul of the party? Not you.
Cold as a pie in a dying man's fridge
is how you feel in these four walls. Because
it's sad, the world, and wrong-headed, a place
you're stuck in waiting for your teeth to go.

You've got the collected symphonies of
Beethoven and Mahler, you've got Mozart.
You've got something going with a woman.
But now you don't see her all that often
and you've no time to listen to music.

You feel like you're stuck between two places
and don't belong in or like either one.
You know you're passionate about something
but half the time you forget what it is
and now and then even what it isn't.

CAPTAIN VALUE

Disappointment at the nth interview.
What it's about, this life, is endurance.

On whose terms is he unemployable?
How will he get his rotten teeth seen to?

He changes razor blades and cuts himself,
the local paper clatters through the box,

he gets the train with the usual bunch
of old people in need of new outfits

who go looking for bargains in Barnsley.
There are plenty but they can't afford them.

SUNDAY WESTERN

The new age travellers who don't travel
are zonked outside the pub in their torn clothes

and I've got a hard-on for a woman
riding a horse in the Sunday Western,

pursued by Indians down a gully.
Old films are always best, unless they're crap.

There are screwed-up beer cans strewn on our path.
They're mine, I threw them there. No one else did.

Harmonica

Wrecking Ball Press, 2003

I WAS AN UNARMED TEENAGER

Sunday morning, just after nine
or just before, and the Salvation Army band
strike up a dirge
right under the window.
I roll my hangover
from one red eye to the other, sit up
and stare down at the musicians
in their uniforms, rasping
their dirty hankie tune-
I shoot them
through their mouthpieces
with an imaginary gun.

My mother's getting warm
in front of an open oven,
a pot of tea just made,
Sunday People on the table
open at the crossword page,
and the dog slobbers toward me
with prisoner's eyes
but he's no chance
of a walk on the canal bank
right now. 'How do you die
like a cowboy,' my mother asks,
"four-three-four?"

BEFORE AND AFTER BREAKFAST

I have to check the furniture
hasn't moved round during the night,
that the bathroom mirror's still broken -
there's a lot of stuff to get done
before breakfast, including forgetting
the dream where I was patronised
across a shiny desk that stretched for miles
by some know-nowt who believes
his life amounts to something.

I go to fetch some bread and milk,
the pavement's full of holes...
I'm wondering what there is
to look forward to.
Breakfast, I guess, and after that,
a film on at midnight-
I've seen it a good few times
but it's worth watching again.
Henry Fonda bites the dust
with a harmonica in his mouth.
You can't help thinking about it,
you can even take it seriously.

JUMBO

I'm not skinny
but this bloke next to me
in the fish 'n' chip shop
makes me look it.
He fondles a roll of
mucky tenners,
slides one out
to pay for his chips 'n' jumbo.
Then this woman glides in
like a slow cat
and the fat bloke winks at me
and says to her,
'Sorry Love, I just bought
the last jumbo sausage.'
He holds it out
right in her face.
'Don't worry,' she says,
peering at it
then meeting the bloke's eyes,
'I've another one just like it
waiting for me when I get home.'
And he's the one who ends up
blushing.
Walking home, eating chips
with my fingers,
I see an empty can
and score a perfect goal.

COLD SPOT

I've taken to wearing
a jacket in the house
it's colder than outside,
the walls are damp,
dripping sometimes,
this is a dump alright,
where I live, fastened in
with the noise of cars
and lorries streaming past,
in my head like harsh voices
or bad music, my breath
steaming up the window
as I stand watching
people without cars,
old, slow, cold, hanging on,
keeping death away
with whatever it takes
and their shopping bags.

I flush the toilet,
hear next door's baby
start to cry. I stand
and listen. It cries and
cries and cries.

SMOKE

The first time I lit up in front of him
it was about midnight,
I was watching The Marx Brothers with Dave.
I was fifteen, Dave was thirteen,
my dad must have been thirty-eight.
I was gagging for a No. 6,
willing my dad to fall asleep
in the chair like he often did.
I think the film was *Room Service;*
something they weren't at their best in.
I stared. I got more and more tense.
In the end I just lit a fag
like it was the most natural thing
in the world for me to do
and my dad
stood very slowly,
walked out and up the stairs
without a word
for months.

THE SLACKER
for David Kennedy

All he's done this summer
is play with dice.
The work was abandoned
like a flat pint.
All he's done is listen
to nobodies
and try to understand
nothing at all.

It's 10 a.m., Sunday
in an old town
where the church bells
won't stay quiet for long.
He's there like chewing gum
stuck to a shoe,
an old brown shoe
in an airless attic.

He stares irresolute
at his bookshelves.
There aren't any new books
he wants to read.
There aren't any old ones
he could re-read.
He selects one
but just can't open it.

TWO LOVE POEMS

(i)
Younger, Fresher
I got my hair cut
this morn ing, too short
is how it looks to me
but she likes it, Jeanette.
She says it makes me look
younger, fresher.
She says it makes me look
as if I know I'm living a life
that could be
much worse.
"Do you like them?" she asks,
turning her feet this way and that
in some new black
high-heeled sandals.

(ii)
Bed Poem
She holds me from behind
or I curl up to her,
I like to feel her warm
backside. Like a workman's
brazier, I tell her.
Go to sleep, she murmurs.
I'm sure someone once said
a poem should be like an
onion, peeling it, layer after layer
bringing tears to the eyes,
but who'd want to wake up
in bed with that person?

SPLINTER

i.m. Mona Eileen Hattersley, 1935-1998

She said it was too small for her to see
and too small for my dad to see
but she had a splinter in her finger,

it was driving her up the wall -
this was when she was about fifty-five
so I was about thirty-four.

She passed me a pair of tweezers,
told me to take the splinter out
if I could see it. I could see it alright

and I got it with the tweezers
and pulled it straight out, no messing,
and my mother gave a sigh of relief.

Eight years later she was full of cancer,
drugged up, surrounded by cards and flowers,
fussed over by strangers in uniforms.

We took her home for the last month, she insisted.
'They can't make a proper cup of tea here,' she said,
'it's no wonder everybody's badly.'

MY SHOES NEED CLEANING

I am the ultimate slacker,
it says so in a review

written by a man who puts Dr.
at the front of his name.

And then I stuff the magazine
in the bin and wonder

if I should cut my fingernails
or merely roll a cigarette.

I do work for a living, though.
Nobody there calls me Dr.,

nobody calls themselves Dr.
I guess nobody's a Dr.

THE 41 GREATEST LISTS OF 41

41 Excuses That Were Never Used
The 41 Greatest Chapter Twos
41 Catchphrases To Make Thee Titter
41 Scotsmen With A Chip On Their Shoulder
41 Famous People With Size Sixteen Feet
41 Dead Men Who Used To Eat Meat
41 Aviators Who Were Scared Of Flying
41 Politicians Who Were Caught Out Lying
41 Picassos That Turned Out To Be Fake
41 Geniuses Who Disappeared Without A Trace
41 Ways To Make A Fool See Sense
The Top 41 Clowns Living In Tents
41 People Who Forgot To Check The Loopholes
41 Men Who Chose Not To Have Balls
The 41 Best Inner Sleeves of 1974
41 People Who Went Through The Green Door
My Favourite 41 One-Armed Drummers
41 Places To Avoid In The Summer
41 Plumbers Who Can't Fix A Leak
41 Species That Will Be Extinct Next Week
41 Practical Jokes That Ended In Grief
41 Popular Phrases To Express Disbelief
41 Actors Who Forgot the Script
41 Builders Whose Jeans Actually Fit
41 Policemen Who Died Of Mirth
41 Texans Who Should Have Been Drowned At Birth
41 Country Singers With A Broken Heart
41 Country Singers Who Broke A Different Part
41 Items Never Found Anywhere Except In A Dustbin
41 Unusual Places To Wear A Safety-Pin

The 41 Step Guide To Walking Down The Street
41 Goalkeepers Who Never Kept A Clean Sheet
41 Instructions You Must Follow To The Letter
41 Diseases That Won't Get Any Better
41 Candles on the Child Star's Birthday Cake
41 Women Who Were Burnt At The Stake
41 Ways To Enjoy Vodka and Orange
41 Ways To Enjoy Gin and Orange
41 Ways To Enjoy Whiskey and Orange
41 Poets Who Couldn't Chew What They'd Bitten
41 Lines That Should Never Have Been Written

RANDY NEWMAN ET AL

The five greatest living American Jewish songwriters
Have been in my ears most of the weekend,
they make me feel like chewing my arm off

and that never hurt anyone.
The sixth greatest would have been in my ears as well
only I'm not sure who it is. Maybe Neil Diamond…

The weather is nothing like a woman
or the weather is exactly like a woman.
I suppose it depends on the woman.

I can hardly believe I'm forty-two.
I feel fifteen or twenty-six or thirty-eight
but never forty-two or forty-one.

HARMONICA

The world continues to be mad,
at times seeming to deteriorate
much faster, suddenly worse than ever

and accepted that way, humoured.
In the privacy of his home
he is mad too, playing Chicago blues

on a crappy harmonica
in a shirt he's worn for seventeen days.
He plays the blues till he's done for

then eats some cold pieces of pie, pork pie
and apple pie. No one hears him laughing
at least he doesn't think so.

BEFORE AND AFTER MIDNIGHT

Wasn't *The Doors* a bloody stupid film?
I just laughed my head off at it.
I don't think I've ever liked a film less.

The telly's off, I smoke a cigarette.
Elsewhere, people rip pieces out of each other
in broken rooms that stink,

beer and pig's breath… I decide to phone Nev
in Sweden, years of long-distance friendship
hanging between us like frayed ropes.

We're not in control of our destinies -
how the fuck did I end up here?
he says, I think, something like that.

NINETEEN OR TWENTY PIGEONS

This bright morning in his new apartment
he loves the sunlight striking everything,
smoke from his cigarette rising through it.

If he knew what was expected of him
he'd surely achieve it, a day like this,
alive and well behind the huge windows.

He stares at the pigeons on the rooftop
of the bakery below, tries to count them.
He wipes sleep from his eyes though he's already washed.

He can clearly recall a hot summer
when he looked like a corpse and felt like one.
All he desires is a boiled egg sandwich.

THE PLAN

I had a plan, of sorts, listen to this-
I'd get myself nailed to a wooden plank
like the saddest bastard who ever lived.

I was crazy no doubt, but how crazy
do you have to be before people realise?
There were crazier people on the loose.

I was proud of my plan, it seemed enough.
I was trying hard to concentrate
but my mind kept drifting off

to imaginary punk blues anthologies
and metaphysical Western movies,
sometimes starring Burt Lancaster.

HIS CHILLING THOUGHT

At least his boat had come in money-wise.
At least he didn't have to work any more.
At least he'd been spared that.

At least he was living:
he could steam the windows up with his smoky breath
which was all the proof he needed.

At least he wasn't a washed-up country singer.
At least he had no less than six good pairs of shoes.
In fact, these really should have been

the best days of his life, the happiest.
Perhaps they were; it was a chilling thought
that un-nerved him as he buttered some toast.

AT THIS TABLE

I stare at the letter. It's from a young poet
who wants advice on how to get gigs in New York,
as if I could help him, barefoot and hungover

at this table in Huddersfield, up to my neck in shit.
This was meant to be my way out.
I'm laughing my head off the more I think of it.

I've been staying out of the sun, I get cold sores.
You have to avoid intimate oral contact,
where's the fun in that… Now Jeanette's telling me

about all the shopping trolleys in the canal
and on the bottom, plastic traffic cones.
The ducks appear unruffled however.

HER NEW BIKER

He grins through his stubble
and offers her another line
and she's not somebody who'd turn it down

because it's good to feel stronger, less real
and break the harsh routine
for a short while.

She plays the new album
by The Red Hot Chili Peppers
to make him feel at home

and sets a mug of steaming tea
on the table, next to his crash helmet
and gloves and paraphernalia.

UNRECALLED MELODY

How come I feel like a blues guitarist
for whom the music has grown stale,
who can't recall the melody he was whistling

when he started the day with a glass of whiskey,
who always talks about himself in the past tense?
It's one a.m., very quiet,

it's hot, my head is hot, my hands.
I sit at the table with the lights off,
there are three huge windows to look out of.

There are places where people are working,
illuminated like poultry farms.
People dying, listen, begging for life.

HER QUESTION

"Now what are we going to do?"
She'd asked the same question
till she was sick of saying it.

He kicked a small stone, sending it
twenty yards; a good shot,
he thought, bloody good shot.

He reached out to hold her hand then.
"I don't know," he replied,
"what we're going to do."

He was all out of ideas.
He'd lifted the lid, found the jar empty.
He'd poked around in it and there was nothing there.

A TERRIBLE SONG

Was just starting. I switched it off
a went to buy a loaf. I had the usual
small worries, sleeplessness
and being at the mercy of dentists,
fourteen hundred tons of job
and the chance I might drop dead
before crawling out from under it,
the possibility of reincarnation
as a business man's fat cigar,
forever puffed on half-smoked in mean lips.
Like someone trying to escape through a porthole
getting their backside stuck, that's how
I felt, and that's not all, there was
a fresh bunch of flowers
tied to the bus stop down the street
again, a fresh bunch of flowers
is tied to the bus stop every Sunday.
I don't know why, I don't know
if I want to know. I don't know much
these days, but I do at least know
a terrible song when I hear one.

SMALL CHOCOLATE HEART

Estimated Cycle Time: 58. 8

The Press opens
I open the gate
remove the mould
I spray the tool
shut the gate
I push the green button
the press closes
I trim the mould
I pack the mould

Instructions To Operator:
Remove Feedgates Flush
Check Each Shot For
Pulling And Plucking

The press opens
I open the gate
remove the mould
I spray the tool
shut the gate
I push the green button
the press closes
I trim the mould
I pack the mould

It's ten in the morning
sunny and warm outside
I'm wearing tight shoes

The press opens
I open the gate
remove the mould
I spray the tool
shut the gate
I push the green button
the press closes
I trim the mould
I pack the mould

Remember: The Next Inspection
Is By The Customer

The press opens
I open the gate
remove the mould
I spray the tool
shut the gate
I push the green button
the press closes
I trim the mould
I pack the mould

Nine hours fifty-six minutes
four point eight seconds
to go

The press opens

THE DEPTH

Management. Two of them
and a couple of young lackeys
are in my way for half an hour
discussing the depth of the mould
coming out of the LB350
every 47.9 seconds .
"They won't wear it. I know
They won't."
"But anything less and it would
fall off."
I stop listening, try to carry on
As if they're not
present, as if I'm not,
as if I was under a parachute
gliding in a blue sky.
Then they are gone.
Our Quality Control Inspector
strides over.
"And what pearls of wisdom
did that lot have for you?"
They were talking, I tell him, about
the depth of the mould.
"The depth?" he says. "*The depth?*"
He turns, walks back to his office
shaking his head.
"They haven't got
a clue. Haven't got
a buggerin' clue."
It's the sort of job where you lose
something, something
you spend the weekends
looking for with tired eyes.

TWO HOURS AND ONE MINUTE

10.57 a.m.
Someone lobs a sprue at me
across the top of some boxes,
missing my head by inches.
I think it was Frank.
It could have been Orville.

12.13 p.m.
I open my bag
to get a banana;
it's been stuffed
with corrugated cardboard,
empty crisp packets,
used plastic cups,
etc.

12.19 p.m.
Jacko appears
right in my face:
"If you *ever*
do anything like that again
I'll pull your bollocks off."
I watch him walk away.
I don't know what I did.

12.58 p.m.
I spot Orville
leaning across a stillage;
I grab a sweeping brush,
cross forty yards in no time,
and jab him up the arse
with the handle.

COWBOY

No one's quite sure how old he is
and he doesn't *let* on
but my guess is sixty-one,
he's Worked here all his life, he says,
since he was seventeen,
"and I haven't got a pot to piss in."
He wears cowboy boots and thick leather belts,
blasts country 'n' Western
from his cassette Player all day.
"Yee-ha!" the others shout, "Yee-ha!"
He just grins, keeps quiet
like a grey-haired outlaw
with nothing left to prove.

One morning he asks me
what a paedophile is.
"Go away;" I mutter.
I walk over, tell Frank.
"Hey," Frank shouts, "Cowboy,
what's all this about you
becoming a paedophile then?"

POWDER MAN

"Fuck off!" he shouts.
"Get fucked!" I shout back.
It's how Jacko and I
say hello every day,
it keeps him happy
and amuses me too.
He's the powder man
who keeps the machines going,
it's a back-breaking job.
He prowls the factory
with a head full of films
like *Full Metal Jacket*,
punching things as he goes,
people if he's that way out.
In a U.S. Marine haircut
he'll say, "Outta the way, Buddy."
His neck's thicker
than some girls' waists.
"I'd shag any woman,"
he informs me,
"except for one."
He doesn't say
which one.

HUMPHREY BOGART

How do you get through life
without knowing who Humphrey Bogart is?
I've been thinking about him for weeks
and mention him to Gary
while we're walking to work.
"Humphrey What?" he says.
I laugh, can hardly believe it,
but it turns out he won't watch anything
on the telly in black and white.
So I tell him Bogart
was Rick, Sam Spade, Marlowe, Harry Morgan,
that he was a guy with lines
and knew how they needed to be said.
He likes that, and takes off his dark glasses
to show me a black eye,
tells me him and his mates
got in a scrap Saturday night,
that he started it, just simply
thumped some geezer without warning.
Why'd you do that? I ask.
"He was a fatso. I don't like fatsos."

NO CHANCE

It's summer, and I stare
from where I'm stuck
trimming moulds for chocolate dog bones
across the floor at Ken,
who's fifty-seven,
who had a heart attack four years ago
during his dinner break.
There he is at the Fourteen Hundred,
hoisting hot, sharp, heavy fans,
sweat staining the back of his shirt
like a lake on a map, pouring down
his flushed forehead and face
and off the end of his nose.
He shakes his head and a thick spray
flies from his hair.
I can't watch too long, have to look away,
have to get on with my own work
which is just as tough
in this sort of heat.
I think if I had a heart attack
they wouldn't get me back in here
at gunpoint. That's obvious.
I wonder what Ken was scared of
and frown.

SUMMER SICK NOTE

We've got lavender toilet paper
made in Worksop
dinner is in the oven
oven is in the kitchen
I'm in the living room
watching the traffic
an endless procession
all sorts of vehicles
here on this road to Blackpool

a young black guy
in a red convertible
his shades reflecting
the bright morning sun
there goes someone with a canoe on their roof
another with a dog at the wheel
and one with a human head
stuck on the bonnet
it's going to be a hot day

my brother Dave is in Sweden
my great friend Nev, he's there as well
I'm not getting much done
watching the traffic from this chair
but it beats the factory
beats it hands down
a bad case of the runs, I told them
it feels great to be here
with no clothes on

ALEX

I don't feel great
about the job I do
but I've got to
feel better than Alex.
On the Fourteen Hundred
making TP9 fans -
they're huge, heavy, very hot moulds
you can barely handle -
he suddenly shouts
"I HATE THIS BASTARD JOB!"
then places his hand
palm down on the table
and whacks it hard
with a five-pound hammer.
It's the second time
he's broken a hand.
Previously, he punched
a concrete post.

BAD ATTITUDE

We each took turns
to pick a cardboard box
up off the floor,
take three self-conscious steps
in slow motion
and put it down again,
and six months later
the Works Manager
gave us fancy certificates
saying we'd attended a course
in Manual Handling.
After I'd stopped laughing
the Works Manager told me
I'd a bad attitude;
he stood gaping
like I was something odd;
'but you turn up on time,'
he added, 'and do your job,'
and then he smiled
and I smiled
and he walked back to his office.

RIDE

To be honest, I didn't care for him,
but was prepared to accept his offer
of a lift home after work in his car.

Talking to him was like selling snails from door to door
so I stopped, listened instead to the latest dance stuff
on his loud radio. I could just about stand it

after the noise of the machines all day,
the minutes and hours gone for good
with the whiff of sweat and the voices of bosses.

Steve was twenty years old and the word was
he'd never done it with a girl.
I smiled and said thanks for the ride.

SPLIFF

When he wakes up he's forty-one years old
and the heatwave appears to have ended
like a tricky piece of oboe music.

Only seven o'clock and already
the noise of vehicles and industry
and he can't be bothered to wash or shave.

He makes a spliff, mean with the tobacco,
sits and smokes it at the kitchen table.
He's suspecting he'll be late for work

yet feels completely at ease, staring
at the traffic without noticing it
and without it noticing him.

JOY

A young Sikh with a grin drives the taxi.
"I bet there's some joy and rejoicing
going on in there this Sunday morning,"
he says as we arrive. I laugh at that
and pay him and get out, moving
slowly, clock in and go to my machine
where the night shift operator
looks just about ready to climb the wall.
He's something of a smackhead, I've been told,
and I believe it, he's certainly weird.
But who on this planet isn't,
and aren't I working seven till seven
every Saturday and Sunday
and taking taxis to the stinking place?

I've dropped on for an easy job today
but stupidly have brought nothing to read
and have to scrounge round for something. I get
The Sunday Mirror, the *Sport on Sunday*
and Friday's *The Sun,* and I read all three
at great length, God help me, I read all three.

POEM MENTIONING ADOLF HITLER

This isn't a hard luck story
though its true these moulds are so hot
they burn my hands when I touch them
and I'm gasping for a smoke.
This isn't a hard luck story
but I made the mistake of telling Jed
that I didn't like Spurs
"Adolph didn't like them either," he said
and winked, and it occurred to me
it's important to have a good reason
for disliking something.
This isn't a hard luck story
because the afternoon goes quick
with Creedence Clearwater Revival
blasting out from Jimmy's table,
carrying fifty yards,
loud enough to be heard
over ten huge plastic injection moulding machines.
This isn't a hard luck story.
We breathe, we press buttons, we drink coffee,
we sweat and complain and blow our noses.
We're here making money for someone else
and a little for ourselves too.

Y'KNOW WARRAMEAN?

Everything he tells you
he follows with the phrase
Y'know warramean?
He's used to drinking every night
Y'know warramean?
I don't mean he goes out every night
he might just have a few cans in the house
Y'know warramean?
If he could get out of the habit of drinking every night
then he wouldn't have to drink every night
Y'know warramean?
And you feel like grabbing hold of him and shouting
I'M NOT THREE YEARS OLD, OF COURSE I KNOW
WHAT YOU MEAN
Y'KNOW WARRAMEAN?
But you don't do that and he carries on
Y'know warramean?

He can't do overtime at the weekends
because of his Community Service
Y'know warramean?
He got done for almost nothing
well they called it assault
Y'know warramean?
I mean you can't call it assault
all he did was shout at her in the street
Y'know warramean?
Well she told the coppers he hit her
Y'know warramean?
Well he might have pushed her slightly

Y'know warramean?
It's o.k., the Community Service
it'd be o.k. if you were getting paid
Y'know warramean?

BOSS ARSE

I almost got the sack
I almost thumped a man
for the first time in twenty years,
a short fat strutting man
who thinks he knows who he is
and who I am, but who knows
less than corrugated cardboard
cut into strips, put in a pile,
less than rusty blades in a tin.
I can hardly believe he's real.
I could hardly believe him real
even as I shook my fist in his face -
"Fuck off you fucking little cunt!"
I should have been cooler somehow,
I should have been something like a freezer;
all afternoon I behave like someone
treading round a puddle of oil,
and the odious little man
still exists, scheming
in a brightly-lit office.

LEE'S DOG

Lee brought his dog to work
because his dad had gone away
and the dog didn't like
being alone all d ay.
Christ, I said, it's a dog,
it doesn't have to like it,
what's it going to do,
pack a suitcase and leave?
Lee tethered it
outside the back door, right next
to where he was working
on the reject mouldings
granulating machine.
It was a huge, stupid-looking beast,
just the sort of dog
a halfwit like Lee would go for,
and it lay on its belly
in the sun all day
with its ugly tongue
lolling from its mouth.
Every time I ducked out
for a cigarette
the dog would be there.
I didn't come even close
to liking it
or anything like that.

RACE RELATIONS ON THE SHOP FLOOR

We had a Young Asian man start
he only worked three or four days.

He sliced his thumb pretty badly
trimming lawnmower underdecks.

There was a lot of blood
all over the table and floor.

I stood looking at it with Lee.
It was our job to clean it up.

Lee said he was surprised there was so much .
"Pakis don't like to part with owt, do they?"

For a while we had two Asian workers
known to most as "The Quiet Paki"

and "The Gobby Paki"
but they didn't last long either.

TWO VERSIONS OF A CARTOON STRIP

1

'DON'T DRINK THAT' the Works Manager shouted
as I took the plastic cup of coffee

out of the machine, raised it to my lips.
I was so shocked I dropped the cup.

'DON'T DRINK THAT BLOODY POISON!' he shouted
and turned and ran away.

I thought he'd finally flipped his lid
and imagined him being bundled out

ranting and raving in a straightjacket.
It was a funny thought, I grinned at it.

2

The Works Manager is in a right flap,
the upper management
furious in their suits.
It seems the drinks machine has been tampered with,
the water tank topped up
with cheap brandy.
I'm loving every minute,
working close enough to the drinks machine
to see everything happening,
but I have to try and look grim.
I try, but can't quite manage it.
"I suppose you find all this amusing,"
the Works Manager snarls.
I should get an award
for not bursting out laughing.

CHICKEN BONE CHARLIE

The three lads in the bus station
aer just about legless, shouting 'Barmy Army'
over and over
as we wait for the
Marsden Hard End. It's 7.28
on a Saturday evening. I'm on my way home
from work, a hard job made harder today
by the close company of Chicken Bone Charlie
a scruffy-arsed little ragamuffin
who got on the wrong side of me
first thing in the morning
by playing a 90-minute Meat Loaf cassette
at full volume on his ghetto blaster.
We didn't speak from 7.15 a.m. to 6 p.m.,
despite working side by side. Then I said,
'Only one hour to go,' and he replied,
'Good. I'm sick of having to look at you.'
So I said, 'Even your best friend
must be sick of looking at you',
then neither of us
spoke again, as the last hour
dragged its heavy feet.

THINGS SUDDENLY LIVEN UP

There was no first-aid man
the Sunday afternoon
Winston caught his wrist
with his trimming knife.
We wrapped yards of bandage
as tightly as we could
while the supervisor
became hysterical.

The nearest hospital
was Huddersfield. I had to navigate
while the supervisor drove.
We were all over the road.
Poor Winston in the back.
He didn't make a sound
all the way there. Blood still seeped through
the layers of bandage.

We left him in Casualty
and drove back to the job.
The supervisor was stricken
but I couldn't help grinning.
It had been a good hour
of unexpected excitement.

LIKE HARPO MARX

*I spend my time standing in places like this
to make me the money that buys me the thing that are
my things once I've bought 'em, not some other fucker's.*

You're beaten if you take it home with you -
the job, all the bullshit.
You try to think about something better

but you can't help going back to *the place*.
I just die there, trying hard not to scream,
nodding my head like Harpo Marx.

*I found out who it was did me house over.
They're in jail for car theft. Soon as they're out
I'm going to smack six shades of shit out of 'em.*

THE HANDSHAKE POEM

The Summer's here and the Managing Director
has just cleared out his desk, looking shaken
to be sacked for incompetence, and with rumours
of financial shenanigans and back-handers
laughed about openly on the shop floor.

Last Christmas, he handed me a large box
of Cadbury's Milk Tray and said, glancing
at the name patch on my pale blue workshirt,
"Merry Christmas, Geoff", and shook hands with m
as though we were sealing a weapons deal.

And then, after catching me outside with a fag
when I should have been trimming lawnmower handles,
my first fag for three, nearly four long hours,
he gave me, some time in April or May,
my third written warning for misconduct.

The summer's here, and the Managing Director
has left the premises, his tail between his legs.
"They say he took ten grand from some Germans…"
We're all sure he's guilty, even if they prove him innocent.
Nothing could mar our ebullient mood.

ONGOING

It's strange to stand here
doing the most mundane job invented.
I've become a dab hand
with a very sharp knife.
There's time to fold my arms
and reflect as I wait for the machine
to complete its cycle
on how dull it is to do this.

We're treated like schoolboys.
There's a list of things we can't do.
No smoking. No eating.
No reading. No crosswords.
No lounging on the tables
as it presents a slovenly image
and damages the tables too.
We need permission to go for a piss.

It's strange to stand here
while share prices vacillate
and while marine biologists
eat sandwiches on warm beaches
and while cats stalk sparrows
in overgrown gardens
and while movie stars make movies
that are nothing like life.

I DID BRAIN SURGERY ON A BARNSLEY PUB FLOOR

Wayne by the juke-box lost an eye at the weekend,
Wayne watching Wayne and Wayne playing pool broke both arms—
he was complaining he couldn't wipe his backside.

Wayne walked in with a dog's skull in the palm of his hand—
"Alas poor Wayne, my fair sister," he said.
He sat down at the bar, in between Wayne and Wayne.

Wayne proposed a toast to Wayne, but Wayne, Wayne and Wayne
refused to drink and left in a bit of a huff.
"John Wayne films! I bloody well can't stand them!"

shouted Wayne, the uninjured one with the moustache.
I took my scalpel out and introduced myself -
"Hello, I'm a surgeon of some renown, Dr. Wayne…"

MEMORABLE AFTERNOON AT THE CINEMA

The new director's cut of *The Wild Bunch*
has brought us here, DK and I. It's very good
at making old stuff seem new, and at the end

when the outlaws take on the Mexican soldiers
imagine our surprise as it becomes clear
bullets are leaving the screen, members of the audience

screaming as chunks of flesh and blood burst from their bodies
in slow motion. We have to throw ourselves to the ground
as a few rounds from Lyle Gorch head our way.

"That Peckinpah!" says DK as we leave,
shaking his head, grinning at all the blood
seeping through the left sleeve of my denim jacket.

HIS FINGERNAILS

I told him his hands were someone else's,
it was their fingernails he'd been chewing,
but he just laughed, as if I was joking.

So I pulled out a large brown envelope,
photographic evidence and so on,
dropped it on the table in front of him.

He stared at it and then he picked it up.
I tapped my feet and hummed 'Smokestack Lightning'
as he tried to take it all in, and then

he was sobbing and my arm was round him.
There, there, I said, you'll feel better later.
I was lying. He'd never feel better.

POSH

There's certainly been a lot of wine drunk,
most of it by a young man in a suit
strutting about the place like a loud boss-

"Six thousand quid," he bleats, "six thousand quid."
He behaves that way because he's stupid
but stupidity isn't an excuse.

Surely we're not being served lion steaks?
I have to stare again at the packet
as it pokes from the top of the swing bin

and look our hostess's legs up and down
like a cheap hoodlum in a B-movie
as she polishes knobs on her posh new cooker.

THE GUITAR

I can't stand this guitar. It doesn't like me much either.
It is between my hands like a severed limb.
Sometimes I think my fingers must have been severed.

I'm hanging on to the one chord I know.
I need a drummer like I used to need mother.
I'm kicking the table-legs and stamping.

Sometimes I think I must be aurally impaired.
I know what I like when I hear it though.
The problem is, I don't hear it, that's the problem.

I know this chord by heart. I can play it perfect.
I can play it but I can't get off it.
I'd call Bad Musicians Rescue Service if there was one.

THE PHONE CALL

It would be wrong of me not to make the phone call
the phone call I promised I would make at this time
and yet I only stare at the phone, don't use it. '

If the phone rang right now I'd collapse in a heap.
I switch the ringer volume off, replace the phone
and sit back and stare at the phone and wonder.

I put some music on but can't hear it for the phone.
I sit with the lights off among shadows and peace
and the phone on the windowsill like a surly cat.

I am trapped in a courtroom of my own making,
hauled up before the judge, found guilty as hell,
sentenced to receiving no phone calls for twenty years.

RED DUNGAREES

For TVR and Nichola

'Thank God,' she said, 'Friday, some music please,'
and she placed her bare feet on top of mine
beneath the table. She was somewhat hoarse

from shouting all day long, but a few drinks
soon put that right. I put 'Abbey Road' on,
it sounded great. George Harrison had died

the day before. 'I think I may have to
buy some new clothes,' I said, 'and stop smoking.'
They were two things I'd never said before

and her eyebrows went up. I lit a smoke.
'Know any shops that sell red dungarees?'
We sat there drunk and ha-ed and ho-ed and hee-ed.

HOT GLUE

Who wants to sniff hot glue twelve hours a day? Not me,
I can't behave as if it was normal,
I can't sit down and switch the telly on,

watch a Clint Eastwood spaghetti Western
spill beer on the carpet, how can I do any of that
sniffing hot glue twelve hours a day?

I wake up and the house is full of cold water,
the same depth upstairs and down, also on the stairs
I'm up to my navel in it.

It's odd how the cat breathes underwater,
how it behaves as if things were normal,
how its purring isn't muffled.

BIG TURTLE

It was definitely a big turtle,
definitely Colchester it was caught.
In a river, it had scoffed all the fish.

People have been drinking hard all weekend,
I know I have. Blues music clung to me
like smoke round a Mississippi camp-fire

and I needed a shave badly. Today
I need water, and a mission. I need
to find a way to make ends meet, sort of.

This woman gets paid to recline on her sofa,
cracking a whip while naked men do the housework.
'I could do that,' says Stephanie.

SOFA FACTORY

I was following a series
of red-lettered signposts:
SOFA FACTORY,
and an arrow, pointing.
I was wondering
if it said SOFA FACTORY
on every street-corner in town.
Then I came to a yard
with some huge iron gates
and above the gates in red paint:
SOFA FACTORY.

The job was dead easy.
All I had to do
was stick sofa catalogues
into envelopes,
put an address label on the front
and stamp them
second-class postage paid.
I kept looking at the clock.
I kept looking at it
like I couldn't believe it.

There were four of us
at a large table.
The others were young blacks.
One of them asked me
if I was an alky.
He said I had that look
about me.

The other two laughed
and I smiled and said
I couldn't afford to be an alky.
Which seemed to be an answer
everyone could live with.

I DREAMED I BURST BALLOONS

I dreamed I burst balloons for a living
and was my own supervisor.
I worked twelve hours a week

and earned a decent wage.
I was never exhausted, never bored.
I was calm like a yacht

in a sunlit harbour,
calm like a rolling pin
or clay elephant.

My past life had been forgotten
like a dull episode of a cop show.
There were no scars on my body.

NOTHING NOTHING NOTHING

1
You don't play football
with the rest,
you spend sports lessons
up a tree smoking.
You can see two of the three games
but you've no interest in them.
When they're finished
you can drop down,
mingle with the rest
jogging back to school.
There's smoke on your breath
but no one gets close.
No one acknowledges you
even exist.

During the dinner break
you smoke inside, hidden
behind some old gym equipment
in the basement, beneath
the head's office.

2
Eating baked beans
cold from the can
with your fingers
and your girlfriend's fingers,
sipping diamorphine
and cans of Skol,

the world's greatest harmonica player
could walk in the room,
you wouldn't act impressed.
"Scuttle along, fishhead,"
that's what you'd tell him.
You are so cool,
crawling to the toilets
with your girlfriend
riding your back.
It must take a lot of practice
to look so tough
in a leather jacket.
You'll keep the whole block awake
if you feel like it
and why shouldn't you
feel like it?

3

Brooding in the bedroom
while the social worker
pontificates downstairs
with your parents.
You can hear the voices
but can't make out the words
and don't even try.
It's not long
before you are summoned.
You are in big trouble,
that's what they try to get you
to swallow
while you tap the chair-arm

with a biro, three-
four time.
You never shave
and have a kind of beard
which now and then
you scratch.

NOT PRETTY

The black coffee hits him like a slap in the face.
Slowly, very slowly, he colours in a picture
of the previous night. It's not pretty.

Some fresh air would do him the world of good
but taking a stroll's one thing he never does.
He'd rather put his fist through a window

or shoot passers-by in the legs.
He'd rather stare at a man's heart in a glass jar
on the top shelf of a shabby wardrobe.

He can't tolerate it, sweat running down his back.
'Just drink your damn coffee,' he whispers, then louder
'just drink your damn coffee and try to act normal.'

OUR MONICA

For Michael Massey

It's turned yellow, her left nipple.
She stares at it in the bathroom mirror.
She squeezes it, it doesn't hurt. Then

she's daydreaming about a place
where she can go for tea, where she's known as
'Our Monica'. It used to be at the end of the street.

She's been singing in bands since she was seventeen.
That's thirty-three years surrounded by men.
Drummers? Don't talk to her about drummers…

She can still hear her mother's loud, broad voice:
'She plays harmonica, our Monica.
Even at school she was always right musical…'

SLEEPLESS

I woke just after one a.m.
to the familiar sound of a police helicopter
circling over the mill, down the canal.

Naked in the darkness, I stood and watched.
Something seemed to be taking place
beneath the thick, dark trees.

Well, the bastards had ruined my sleep.
I rolled a spliff, just a single-skinner,
some homegrown stuff, smoked it on the sofa

as the coppers hovered,
probing with their stupid spotlight
for any sign of life.

IN A HEATWAVE

Twenty five to bastard seven.
A gathering of men in the canteen
drinking murky coffee from plastic cups,

reading *The Sun* or *The Star* or *The Mirror*
yawning and coughing and cheerless.
I take my place with them.

By eight o'clock I'm drenched in sweat,
juggling red hot rubber dog bones,
and by five pas three I'm barely living. I turn

to the old black guy on the next machine
and tell him I think I'm going to die.
He shrugs – 'Can't say I blame you man.'

AGAINST SUICIDE

People think up the strangest ways
to do themselves in.
I heard of a woman

who did it with clothes pegs.
Then there was a group of young men
who strapped bombs to themselves.

I won't be doing it
with bombs or clothes pegs.
I'd feel too self-conscious,

and I want to live long enough
to see the animated version
of the end of the world.

WITH THE BOSSES

The thought of engaging them
in conversation
makes my skin crawl.
Even so, here I am, speaking
and being spoken to
in a too-bright office.

Why is work always dull or bard
or dull and hard?
Why is there never enough time
to pursue things that make life worth living?

I don't ask these questions, just desire to.
I want to say I like the shift pattern
four days on, four days off
it means only half of your life is shit.

P FOR POEM

I'm tired, slumped in a chair,
struggling to take it in-

aircraft crashing,
buildings collapsing,

dust and smoke and holy shit
everywhere.

Things can only get worse,
I mean better.

Death's boots are shuffling
on the Welcome mat-

'I don't need anything right now!'
I shout.

Back of Beyond

Smith/Doorstop, 2006

The Cigar

The cigar was huge. It was carried in
by three underfed slave-children in chains.

Everything stopped: spoons on their paths to mouths,
footsie under tables, all the soft words.

The President glanced round slowly
with the beginnings of an imbecilic grin…

Before the stunned gapes of the other customers,
he summoned a blow-torch and lit the thing.

It began to expand at an alarming rate,
taking a new, strange form, developing

what seemed to be a head. One woman abandoned
her life's jewellery, collapsed to the ground moaning

'Give it *me*! Give it *me*!' Her husband, tears streaming,
gobbled a photograph of their lovely children.

Waiters rushed to and fro with bowls of hot veal soup,
their bow-ties on the verge of hysteria.

Chandeliers fell crashing; in the darkness,
bottles of wine hopped back to the cellar,

remarkable creatures leapt from their plates,
forked just in time by the sweating manager.

The President celebrated
by loudly eating the whole five-pound lump

of garlic stilton with port wine on the dessert trolley.
The room was small and becoming increasingly

smaller. There seemed no escape

HE WAS CERTAINLY AN INTELLECTUAL

He'd be there, poised with red pen
over the latest collection of Steiner essays,

eager to underline
everything obvious to you or me.

He liked to talk about famous literary figures:
Lawrence, Hardy, Eliot, Conrad, James –

they were all such wonderful people
who'd done such wonderful things.

He could talk for hours and hours.
Hadn't he written twenty-two hundred

letters over the years to *The Observer*?
Hadn't he read *Heart of Darkness*

seventeen times?
He could assure you he had.

CHRISTMAS SHOPPING

You were writing dud cheques
like no one's business,
I was splashing
the forged tenners around.

In the hole in the road
someone sang
'Take Me to Tulsa',
snow settling on his sombrero.
I tossed him a tenner
screwed into a ball.

A woman approached
armed with documents
and truth;
she was selling badges,
a definite bargain
at a tenner apiece.

I signed the petition
to end the war,
I do a lot
of possibly useless writing.

THAT WEEKEND, YOU WORE

a tragic expression and were
loaded with meaningful glances.

We walked along the beach whipped
by sand on the wind, poked
at crabs half-eaten by gulls

and later, on the boating lake,
lost the oars and were forced
to abandon ship in the high wind.

There had to be a toilet
somewhere, but we couldn't find it,
so you disappeared into a bush,

and an old man's eyes grew wide
as he hobbled by – my clothes
dripping wet, a bent fag in my lips,

murmuring sweet nothings to a bush.

BECAUSE

Because his face did not fit
he walked in sideways, on his hands,
pushing a wheelbarrow loaded with groceries.

His moustache sweating, he pogo-danced the bump
toward the bowl of tulips, grabbed a bunch,
ate them noisily while whistling 'Little Stevie'.

He gave piggy-back rides to all the pregnant women.
He impersonated a trout on the end of a hook.
He applauded their insults

because his face did not fit.
And if it's true he didn't 'get the joke',
it's also true the joke wasn't very funny.

READERS

I have readers, they add up
to twenty, and I know at least
five women who're half-impressed.

Think of this: showing a book
by a friend to your mother,
your mother in the apron and slippers.
'He reminds me of you,' she says,
tossing the book aside, 'barmy.'

It can take years to get this far, years.

SHADOWS ON THE BEACH

On the beach at Dahab, the sand was hot.
It felt good to sit there, to be naked
and take things easy, to glance out to where
the women plunged shouting into the sea.
On the radio, Jim Morrison wanted
to be loved two times, Ba-by, loved twice today.

A small Bedouin girl aproached,
a shadow on the pages of my book.
I looked up, smiled. Shyly, she asked
if she could eat the apple-core
I'd just dropped in the sand.

DIARY OF A WEEK IN SEPTEMBER

Don't ask me how
but Sunday never happened.

Monday, I blinked for an instant,
it was suddenly Tuesday.

That's when I fell asleep
while planning for Wednesday.

I woke on Thursday, spent the day
wondering where was Wednesday?

Friday you said was really
Thursday, and before we knew

where we were it was Saturday.
Some things needed dusting

and there was a shopping list
as long as *The Log of the Sloop Exceed.*

THE MAN AT NUMBER TEN

slams his front door:

there goes a man who
takes himself seriously,

shoulders hunched
for passers-by,

always busy
going nowhere, fast.

He spends every Sunday
with his head in an engine,

every single evening
throwing darts at a board.

He seems content
with a dog and a wife,

I've sometimes seen him
take one or both for a walk.

THEOLOGY

A good friend of mine
one day; the next,
someone who just happened
to look like her.

'God tapped me on the shoulder,'
she said
and handed me the leaflet.

Returning home on the bus
I heard one schoolgirl
telling another
'Simon Bletsoe put his hand
on my fanny last night.'

Later, the same one
tapped me on the shoulder
to ask for a light.

ALMOST UNBELIEVABLY

Sad, to be sitting here still
smoking too many cigarettes,
watching this cold pancake of a film
for the third time in one life,

to consider my mother,
patiently sitting through Western
after Western with my father
because she *liked the scenery*.

History repeats itself, after
a fashion, and these also
are facts: the diaries we've kept
aren't worth the paper they're scrawled on,

our stamp collection—
let's face it, it's dull.
When the toast caught fire
last night and the grill,

it was the most exciting event
here for at least three years.

DESERT

We were out in the desert, just sort of
fooling around, dreaming up names for some
loud, long-haired rock band we'd be sure to form
the minute we got back home. I liked most

Doctor Straight Neck and his Toothpick Killers.
That was when Heidi started laughing and
couldn't stop – as much the drink and heat as
the wit, I guess. But it was good, hearing

her laugh like that, after all she'd been through.
The desert could do that. Such stillness there,
as if the earth was taking breath, as if
history was yet to be invented.

I look after cacti in the house now.
They don't take much of that. I never did
keep in touch with any of those people,
though I heard Heidi died in Berlin, smack.

LOVE POEM

Alan hates John and Pete.
Pete hates Alan and John.
John hates Pete but not Alan.
I hate Pete and Alan

and John. Alan hates me.
Pete and John might hate me
for all I know. Nev hates
no one. No one hates Nev, though

the two boys from Dover
hate the lot of us. We hate
the two boys from Dover.
The two girls from Finchley

hate John and would hate Alan
too if they knew he read
their diaries. We all hate
the people we see with

money, the people who buy
groceries. The people
hate us also. I hate
the smell of France and its wine.

DAYS

Our lives in yawning
back-to-backs,
mud and dogshit dragged
across acres of carpet,
so many kettles
boiling and boiled.

It has come to this,
that when we step round
the puddle the rushing car
will spray us head to foot,
that when we smile
at the neighbour she'll say
Who the fuck do you think
you're laughing at?

These are the days
to sit with music:
Jaco Pastorius
re-defining electric bass
as easily as most people
breathe.

TOAST

I worry too much
about the past, silly things:

leaving my mother's
plastic breadbin
on the grill-top
while making toast,

the men who said they'd
kill me before long.

Then there was Israel:
spent cartridges
and blood by the roadside,

and the noise, everywhere.

HOW SHE PUTS IT

'It's about time you grew up,' she says,
as though he doesn't know that theory.

'All I said,' he starts to say
but she's not interested

in all he said, slamming
the door as she leaves.

He's both feet on her coffee table
when she later tells him it's over:

'Get out and take your ugliness with you,'
is how she puts it.

BRIEFCASE

Life makes as much sense to me
as a ripe avocado does to a dog.
I was passed an unsigned cheque
by a man impersonating a friend

and got back home to a cold meal.
I found a man's black leather briefcase
in the corner of the bedroom
and knew it was my own.

THREATENING AT ANY MOMENT TO BLUSH

The girl is telling me she doesn't like
poetry, not really, not much, only
Brian Patten, John Cooper-Clarke and Joolz

and now me. This is new and exciting,
to be signing books for girls just left school
unsure yet how to hold a cigarette

and a half-lager in the same small hand.
I finish with a flourish, and then X,
and the girl stays a while, smiling a lot,

blushing a lot, glimpses of a party
I reckon I'd be happy to gatecrash.
But I stay sober in the face of it,

as though someone had tapped on my shoulder
to whisper, 'Hey, you're a married man, now.'
Which is what happened, more or less.

MEATBALLS, JERUSALEM, TATTOO

The beer was warm but I drank it all the same,
and ate the meatballs, two on a white plate, a little gravy,

while the proprietor offered various photographs of himself,
his sexual acts with European women,

proudly, like showing off family snapshots to a tired colleague,
the meatballs going down slowly, needing to be chewed well.

I saw the tattooed number on the old woman's arm
as I studied Hamsun and Pound in the bookshop.

THE DRUMMER

He claimed to be a drummer
just a drummer

though we couldn't help but notice
the sticks in his hands, the obscenity

the way he'd stare, stare
ahead as he drummed

disturbing with his drums
his *drumming* the neighbourhood

stirring things up, things
best left unstirred, yes

at times *directly polemical*
this this this this drummer.

We could break his hands
and we did break them.

SPIDER

The spider was completely unprepared
for assault from above by an ashtray.

It never had a friend it could count on.
It never knew its blood group.

It never saw itself changing, or any need to.
It never said: 'No more excuses.'

It never felt tempted by drugs.
It never knew the itch to the nearest bar.

Its earning power was never an issue.
It was never hurt by a few home truths.

It never did anything for anyone.
It never knew the myth of Wyatt Earp.

It never hoped for more than was likely.
It never had Watchtower thrust at it.

It never saw a rainbow, or a bunch of flowers
dropped into an open grave.

It never wrote an essay on the works of Alexander Pope.
It never filled in an application form.

It never married for love or money.
It never had a honeymoon in a hotel.

It never knew who was Prime Minister.
It never knew if it was lucky or not.

It never shopped for clothes.
It never smiled.

It never felt like a paperclip
in a jar in a cupboard in a shed.

It never carried a briefcase.
It never missed the last train.

It never slept off a hangover.
It never thought it was Marlon Brando.

It never grew a beard, or shaved in cold water.
It never fished in the Mississippi.

It never heard rumours about itself.
It never had to face its inadequacy.

It never had any wild ideas.
It never had any wild ideas drummed out of it.

It never laughed at a copper's helmet.
It never gave a false name and address.

It never saw the Marx Brothers, or listened to Sgt. Pepper.
It never knew what was in fashion.

It never got careless, or said it was past caring.
It never left its clothes lying in a heap.

It never preferred to remain anonymous.
It never wondered who wrote Shakespeare

or invented light-bulbs.
It never thought it would win an award one day.

It never moved because it didn't like the neighbourhood.
It never fastened its seat-belt for a rough ride.

It never played a guitar that had just one string.
It never looked for warts in its armpits.

It never turned its back on the dreams of its youth.
It never felt guilty for wasting time.

It never considered circumcision.
It never got hard-ons travelling by bus.

It never got sentimental at Christmas.
It never thought the carpet and curtains clashed.

It never spent a night awake with its partner
wishing the photograph album empty.

It never read about itself on the front page.
It never had more than its fair share of problems.

It was never diagnosed manic-depressive.
It was never found guilty of a thing.

It never made a list of things to do.
It never waited for the right partner to come along,

or became half of a couple with a headache between them.
It never dropped earwax in the ashtray.

It never had a first at the races.
It never tied a donkey to someone sleeping.

It never had a pension plan.
It never wanted to impress itself,

or thought it was better than it was.
It never got serious over the funniest things.

It never had a boss for a friend,
or a friend who thought he was a boss.

It never stared out to sea, it never watched the tide come in.
It never worried whether or not it created a good impression.

It never took notice of a roadsign.
It never put a barbed-wire fence up.

It never wept inside headphones, briefly.
It never learned to think things over more,

to peep before it plunged.
It never took its shoes off to save the carpet.

It never learned to spell archaeologist.
It never scratched its arse in a food queue.

It never read a book about Hitler.
It never met a neo-oligarch.

It never used washing powder, or learned to start a fire.
It never used a telephone box.

It never accepted a cigarette.
It never laughed at its own joke.

It never sat in the back row,
or dreamt it was the steering wheel through James Dean's chest.

It never grew its hair to its shoulders.
It never picked its feet on the bed.

It never had a twenty-first birthday party.
It never washed its hands of anybody.

It never needed an explanation, or a diet.
It never said: 'Too gentle for my liking, too jolly.'

It never taught itself German, telling its partner
to be quiet so it could concentrate.

It never worried about what it was swallowing.
It never looked for heroes and villains.

It never smiled apologetically.
It never pressed a blade into its wrist.

It never wished it lived in a caravan.
It never fried bacon and eggs.

It never felt like a fat catalogue
of books published in limited editions

no one wants anyhow, not at any price.
It never tore a book in half.

It never felt like it was an abstract
that has everybody shaking their heads.

It never had a gun held to its head.
It never felt a wire tightened round its throat.

It was completely unprepared
for assault from above by an ashtray.

PROBLEMS WITH THE OVERFLOW

You don't like to lose your cool and you don't
often. If you do, you think of a machine
that moves through the streets chopping legs off at the knees
and now the kids on the corner whistle
the funeral procession as you pass them.
But you're pretty thick-skinned and can take it
and there's always something to keep you from brooding:
a door that won't open or a door that won't close,
an overflow that keeps overflowing
or signs of strength or weakness in a rival.
What do you care if someone else freezes
in a bath they should have emptied?
You listened through the wall as he sang: he was deep
as a country 'n' western compilation
and with the same belief in the double-negative,
crackling like a 78 when he should have been a CD.
If his future was a building it would be demolished
but it's nothing to you since you woke up
and lit a fire – not a large one, about
the size of a copper's helmet or head.

Not far from where you spit, a family play
croquet on the lawn. There's a bright steel skateboard
poking under their gate like a machine.

SLAUGHTERHOUSE

At last, I was ready to say goodbye
to a tether made of fishnet stockings.
My friends told me not to, that I needed
a bandage for my head, needed a crutch for it.
I muttered Jolly Good like a jolly fellow,
caught the next bus. When I got where it was going
a man tried to sell me a Coke for five dollars.
I asked the next for the way to the slaughterhouse.
He told me to follow the smell of blood and bone.
The smell was powerful, at some distance even.
*

The first time I ate grilled octopus tentacles –
a strange moment, one I feel a need to mention.
An undercover cop had leeched onto me at a bar,
between mouthfuls of ouzo and tentacles
was pretending to be the greatest punk rock band ever.
He asked if I wanted to dance, the meathook
in my hand was reassuring. He loved every minute
of his pathetic life. Young men with sticks
surrounded our piled-high table
after he told the barman he should fuck his bill.
*

The morning after I ate grilled octopus tentacles
a man helped me buy powder in the pharmacy,
took me by the arm and found me a hotel room.
I was embarrassed among strangers the rest of the day –
they were passing round photos taken on the beach
that summer I weighed fifteen and a half stone.
At night I searched every room in the place,
sifting through bins stuffed with used tampons and shit-roll

for one small thing that would let me know where I was.
The landlady joined me about half-two.
*

I did press-ups and pull-ups and ran on the spot.
I brushed my teeth and shaved away three months
of enthusiastic cunnilingus.
I practised speaking without using shit and fuck
and held myself erect. Bumping into her on the stairs
I complimented her on her repertoire
but suggested she make more of a noise.
What do I most wish now, as I pick my teeth here
some years later? That she had understood a word I said
and that my nose hadn't been so obviously running.
*

The slaughterhouse started my head pounding
and there is a harsh sound, a hundred cows
screaming in unison. I went nuts there
and then. Years of treatment would have followed
if I hadn't escaped the building that minute.
I hitched a lift with a man who told me
I had good legs, sexy legs. He needed glasses
and a room at a hotel, I replied –
did he have his wallet? Yes he did. His head cracked
as he landed in the road, I didn't look back.
*

What I fell in love with was her singing,
not that it was what you'd call good singing.
It would reach me in my room as I lay naked
in the baked afternoons, talking aloud
to the insects on the ceiling and walls.
It was the happiness that surprised me,
and how it lingered a long time after.

I was never a music critic, no,
Not bad, I'd say, turning this way and that,
looking in the mirror at my pale face.

TROUBLE

He makes no more noise than a cactus plant.
He's closed the curtains and left the lights off.

He knows his enemies won't let it drop.
They'll stick his head on a pole, dance round it.

He's closed the curtains and left the lights off.
He thinks of a room with a door with no handle.

*

They'll stick his head on a pole, dance round it.
He should have listened to what friends told him.

He thinks of a room with a door with no handle.
He'd like that room. He'd like that door a lot.

He should have listened to what friends told him:
You go there with that face you can expect trouble.

*

He'd like that room, he'd like that door. A lot.
The thing he just can't get out of his head's

You go there with that face you can expect trouble.
Nothing's a joke, nothing's funny, nothing.

The thing he just can't get out of his head's
he knows his enemies won't let it drop.

Nothing's a joke, nothing's funny, nothing.
He makes no more noise than a cactus plant.

MINUS THREE POINT SIX

Suppose there are three doors:
Religion, Insanity, Suicide.
Suppose you're on TV,
the hostess asks which door you'll take.
Suppose ten million viewers

and a studio audience of enemies
are all shouting their preference
and in the din the hostess mishears:
you ask for Religion, get Insanity.
You're shoved through and the door closes.

You try to shout for help, you want
to explain there's been a mistake,
you can't, can't move, feel as if
you're held in place by chains
or a pair of huge hands.

It's so dark you can't see yourself,
so quiet you could hear a plant move
though there are none moving.
There are no words in your head, just numbers.
You try but can't stop thinking about them.

One and one is two plus seventeen is eighteen
minus three point six is fifteen point eight
multiplied by twenty-seven point seven is
four thousand three hundred and sixty-five point six
divided by five point five is

HANNON IN A NUTSHELL

His gripe was with the whole world, everybody,
and it seemed no amount of money
would put a smile on that long face.
His seventh album, called *Seventh Album*,
bristled with unresolved grievances,
'The Big Ships' and 'On The Other Hand'
the tracks that attracted most attention.
In the former, a solitary piano chord
repeated at five-second intervals
as Hannon grunted his ex-wife's name
was the sparest rock recording
since the heyday of Haddock Potion.
'On The Other Hand', on the other hand,
was its antithesis, a wild incantation
positively celebrating his loneliness,
the twenty-five percussionists
taking it into uncharted territory.
It is a stunning, twisted performance,
shocking as an amputation, perhaps
completely paranoid.

Hannon's mental decline over the following years
is well-documented elsewhere. Suffice to say
the Nixon Holiday Inn disturbance
was not an isolated incident
and the artistic output suffered correspondingly.
His relevance to the young of today
can be summed up thus: there but for the grace of God
could have gone your dad.

DON'T WORRY

A man in the Elephant and Castle
said there were games I should know more about,
I should try fags on the backs of my hands
or taking a shotgun to bed with me.
I recalled him dropped in the street one night,
the fine crack in his skull, the blood, the cold,
the copper who didn't think he'd make it.
'I tell thee lad, listen, what I don't know
about masturbation's not worth knowing.'
The place was suddenly brighter, I realised
he couldn't see me, he wasn't talking
to me at all. His brother came in then
with the news Clothes Line wouldn't be coming,
they'd been in a pile-up, all their gear
was written off. A girl who followed them
from gig to gig began to shake her head.
'Don't worry,' I told her, 'no one was hurt
except the bass player. His ribs showed through
his blood-soaked shirt as they tried to free him
from the snare drum.' I drank up and set off
along the canal, kicking at loose stones,
whistling one of the old songs I'm sick of,
sometimes stopping to see if I could spit
hard enough to reach the opposite bank.

NOBEL PRIZE POEM

He awoke with no hangover
because he'd had no beer
and looked in the mirror.
He couldn't help noticing
that a box of old records
not worth listening to
teetered on his neck
in place of a head.
He tied his shoelaces.
He was barefoot.
*

At the time, he was seeing
a Scandanavian woman
whose life was her watercolours:
orange skies, pink highways.
She wanted to live in a cave
and win the Nobel Prize.
I'm not interested
in saving the world,
he told her,
it's hard enough remembering
to change my underpants.
*

Then he wrote a story
about a bad writer
and thirty-seven people
sent him insulting letters:
How dare he portray them
in such a callous manner?
He couldn't even remember
meeting fourteen of them.
Three or four of them
were actually good writers.

ECCENTRIC HAIR

There was something grinning on the telly:
Everything's creative, it said, meaning
staring at a shadow on the ceiling.
I didn't switch off, just sort of grunted.
I wasn't good for much at the time
except worrying about the first post
coming ten minutes after the second,
the cop who parked outside my house reading
How The CIA Murdered Bob Marley
and the gangsters who tailed me when I went
to the bank, to the shops, to the dentist.
I was low, listening to the same song
over and over: *Don't Tell Me You Don't Believe It*
                                & Call Yourself A Friend
and I'd no idea what I wanted,
other than to be able to relax
and see the funny side of things again,
maybe think back to being seventeen,
wishing I was Bob Dylan or someone
or at least had pretty eccentric hair.
I just needed to get out more, out of the house.

My suit was at the drycleaners so I wore jeans
and a denim jacket. I leaned against the bar
avoiding the eyes of the other customers:
the place was full of all the fools I'd ever been.
I heard them getting more and more maudlin.

HYPHEN

The party was like the hyphen in Seymour-Smith.
The men were a stiff bunch, the women even worse.
I ended up pretending I'd the shits:
'Must have been the meat, I'm not used to it.'
We needed great mouthfuls of air, walked rather than
take a taxi. Jeanette took her shoes off
and her feet got dirty. She washed them in the sink
while I picked up a book. I read aloud,
it was pretty funny. You know the book I mean.
There was a lot of noise outside: dogs, screams,
and Jeanette came and peered through the curtains,
leaving a trail of damp, talcumed footprints
which I pointed out when she turned back round.
'When are you going to get your clothes off?' she said.

ELSECAR RESERVOIR

Although languid on the surface
Elsecar reservoir is dangerous
to swim in. Underwater currents
can grab and drag you down
into a system of potholes.

I hear myself say this
and can hardly believe it.
Jeanette turns away, startled.
Old people are feeding ducks,
a few fishermen sit still.

Pike are another reason
for not swimming, I say.
They've been known to swallow
whole men, boys anyway,
let's put it like this –

It's looking like rain
says an old man with a cap
and a dog that cowers.
It weren't forecast though
he adds as he passes.

Let's put it like this,
you definitely wouldn't want
to go swimming with the fuckers.
I stop and sit on the bank,
feeling in my pocket for my fags.

One of the fishermen pulls in
a strange object, nothing
like a fish. Everyone
stands around discussing it
as it flip-flops on the bank

then suddenly it's down the bank and gone
before anyone can stop it.
Two girls aged four and six
start to cry in the next street.
We can hear them clearly

till the brass band starts up.
That's funny, Jeanette says,
I can hear a brass band
but I can't see it.
Seventy-Six Trombones is what they play.

IN PHIL'S BUTCHERS

They're sure they know me from somewhere:
'Aren't tha t' bloke that rode naked
on a bike through Jump for charity?
Thi picture wa' in t' Chronicle.'
The previous customer leaves, coughing
something red and green onto the pavement.
'That's a poorly mister, dead on 'is feet 'e is.'
One of them decides he worked
with my brother at Johnson's
though I've no brother who worked there.
'Are tha sure?' he wonders.
An older man (is it Phil?)
pops his head in from the back room:
'Leave t' lad alone 'n' gi' 'im 'is pies.'
I hold them in my hand as I say 'Ta-ra'
and leave, taking off my dark glasses.
There's a patch of blue sky
where my eyes should be, which startles
an old woman crossing the road.
'By,' I say, to reassure her,
'it's cold enough for a walking stick.'
'All laughter is despair,' she replies,
'it's t' human condition, like.'

REMEMBERING DENNIS'S EYES

He always blinked too much,
like an overnight guest who leaves
with the toilet paper in his holdall
or leaves a dry blanket
covering a wet bed.
Even with the balaclava
turned round to hide his face
I could see him blinking
through the makeshift eyeholes.

Gimme the bastard bag
he yelled, tugging at it.
The iron bar bounced on
the guard's helmet five times
before he fell to his knees,
another four or five before
he lost his grip on the bag.
Tha saw nowt, nowt, Dennis hissed,
pinning me to the wall
with one hand, waving the bar
like a conductor with the other.

The last time I saw him,
years later, years ago,
he'd just tried to strangle his ex-wife,
had been stopped by
his ten-year-old daughter.
He was running toward Darfield
like a wind-up toy
with a pair of kitchen scissors
sticking between his shoulder-blades.

DEATH'S BOOTS
for Ian McMillan

In a previous incarnation, I climbed mountains
and sang my own praises, anticipating the trend.

On each wall of my home hung gaudy self-portraits.
I was posing for the camera before I invented it.

Then I was told I was a fool, that my career was over
for perfecting the ever-lasting light-bulb.

So I took a post kicking the oats out of farmers.
The money was good. Death's Boots, they called me.

I became involved because I saw no reason not to.
The reasons would pile up later like wood-shavings

from the pencils of the man who wrote *The American Century*.
That man was me, Death's Boots.

THE ONLY SON AT THE FISH 'N' CHIP SHOP

He lived with his mother till he was forty-five
and no one was allowed to touch his head.

He worked on a novel for twenty years
without writing a word. He didn't like people

who wrote novels. He often drank. One glass of beer
was too many, two glasses weren't enough.

Travel brochures were as far as he went.
A football match, one time. He often said

'Why would anyone want to think about a potato?'
He painted his door with nobody's help.

THE PERSUADERS

A well-known nobody
is opening The Countryman in Wombwell
and some people are ridiculous enough
to turn up and ask for his autograph.
He's ridiculous enough to sign them.
Twenty years on, we sit arguing

over who it was: Tony Curtis? Or
Roger Moore, before he was James Bond?
The beer's warm and a rockabilly band
are trying to pretend electricity
hasn't been invented. The harmonies are great
if you like that kind of thing. When we leave

the six of us walk in single file
up the narrow street that takes us
past The Angler's Rest and The Ship
and the Conservative and Catholic clubs
and British Legion and Royal Oak
and The Alma and Little George
and into the Horse Shoe,
where the barmaid is a comedienne:
'Good evening, ladies and beasts.'
It's Nev's round.

ON THE BUSES WITH DOSTOYEVSKY

Because of the steelworks
that deafened my dad
our telly was always
too loud, so loud
it formed a second narrative
to what I was reading
up in my room
in my late teens – I'd have
Hemingway and *Kojak*,
Alias Smith and Jones and Poe.
All that noise! Car chases
and gunshots, sirens, screams,
horse racing and boxing,
adverts for fish fingers,
floor cleaner and fresh breath;
and Knut Hamsun starving,
Ahab chasing his whale.
I felt like a learner driver
stalled at a traffic light,
a line of lorries behind me.
Because of the steelworks
that closed in 1970
I like silence and calm,
I like silence and smoke
cigarettes in the dark.

GRACE

died in a hospital bed
surrounded by her family.
She'd been unconscious
days on end
then suddenly sat up and
looked her husband
right in the eye.
They were both
eighty-three.

I sat there
a while, just her and me.
I wanted to believe
somehow, somewhere, something
Of her still lived.
I held her hand,
recalled a dream I'd had
when I was four.
Grace saved me from a lion,
beating it off with a poker
at the top of the cellar steps.

HOLY AIR

I

This is where Jesus died and was reborn.
It's illegal to drive a bus unarmed
and the drivers wear side-holsters,
strut round the station like a posse.
A dozen soldiers share the seats with you,
nursing their rifles, never letting go.

This is where Jesus was resurrected
and the bazaars are full of it.
You need money, a lot,
and Arabs will follow you down the street –
'I can sell you a jar of Holy Air
at a reasonable price.'

II

'This street is closed,'
says a young Arab boy
suddenly blocking my path,
'bad muslims.'
He holds out his hand
and I give him a shekel
as the call to prayer
rolls across the rooftops.
God is great! he shouted
as he detonated the bomb
strapped to his chest.
Something like this happens
and does not stop.

NOT FOR AESTHETIC

I'm to work with Mario,
an Argentinian carpenter
who's been on the kibbutz
six years. He arrives
on a bicycle, a white Labrador
trailing behind. With winter
peeping round the corner,
it's important we paint
the outside of some new
wooden buildings. 'Not
for aesthetic, but to…'
He blinks behind his glasses
and waves his hands.
'Protect,' I say.
'Yes,' he says.
Today though the sun is hot
and I take off my shirt,
can feel my back roasting
as I slap grey paint.
It's hard to believe
it's November; back home
they'll be buttoning big coats,
wrapping their scarves.
But Mario insists
that here too it will be cold
and raining before long.
He constantly apologises
for his English:
'I study it five years
two hours each week

but I never speak it.'
Really I have no trouble
understanding him, though
he doesn't seem to get
much of what *I* say.
'It's my northern accent,'
I tell him, 'we're poor
and can't speak properly.'
'In Argentina, the south
poor and the north…'
'Prosperous.'
'Yes.' And later,
the work done, walking home,
Mario pushing his bicycle
and the dog trotting
alongside, nosing the grass
for lizards or hedgehogs,
I try to tell him more
about the north of England –
the pits shut, the unemployment,
Thatcher's legacy.
'In my country,' he says,
'we call the Malvinas
Thatcher's war.'
The dog runs barking
to the foot of a tree.
'In mine too,' I reply
in my clearest English.
He nods, and shouts something
at the now frantic dog.

NOVEMBER

The young Israelis
accept their lot.
Here at this kibbutz breakfast table
are a dozen, boys and girls
who'll soon be soldiers.
And the long hair of the boys,
hanging over the backs
of their Jim Morrison
and Nirvana t-shirts,
or tied in ponytails,
and the rings through the noses
of the girls and some boys,
will go, must go, in March.
November, they sit
cheerfully eating eggs
and reading their newspapers
back to front, left to right:
five soldiers wounded slightly
near the Lebanese border;
one killed in a drive-by shooting
in the quiet town of Safad;
three killed, one left paralysed
by a suicide bomber
at Netzarim junction.
This is the daily news.
And I sit with them
and chew toast and jam,
thirty-eight and British
and safe, and wonder if
any will make the news
themselves.

PIPER

At the age of thirty-seven
he owns only what he stands in
and enough stuff to fill a duffel bag
but he's not worried.
He stopped worrying about the future
the day he left Germany
to avoid the draft,
losing himself in Amsterdam
with a woman who could keep up.
He made a living.
The day the police arrested him
he had a ticket to see Dylan –
for more than one decade
this had been an ambition.
Instead, he got to spend two years
reading Albert Camus and Herman Hesse,
Charles Bukowski and Jack Kerouac.
It was like being back
in the orphanage.

Pale and skinny, hardly
a word to say for himself.
We see him quickly change
into a muscular, tanned raconteur,
holding court on his porch
all afternoon and evening
until something, the past
or some version of the future,
puts a bottle of vodka
firmly in his hand,
clouds his eyes.
And he's turning up for work drunk,
seven in the morning.

SOMETHING FROM A STUPOR

He held a bottle of Gold Star up,
peered into it solemnly.
Told me for the tenth time
he was just 'one of the guys',
something reptilian
about the stare he fixed me with
through the green glass of the bottle.
He was young enough to be a son
I'd disown,
the sort of man who'd rip
somebody's photo to pieces.
He glanced from face
to face, grinning;
the two fat blokes at our table
left with their expensive cameras.
'We don't need them,' he said, and
laughed, 'I don't need anybody.'
Then the noise started, the disco,
and he was off and dancing,
leaving behind his untouched beer
and a smell like gunpowder.
I saw him only one more time, a glimpse,
just before the place closed
at five in the morning,
of a small group of men his own age
herding him through the door,
his cries
drowned out
by 'Trenchtown Rock'.

THEY WERE BOTH LIARS

Boring as well, though the girl
falling out of the window
story was at least
energetic. The eldest
was drunk, an idiot half the time,
unconscious the rest.
'You don't like to talk to me,' he said,
vodka in my face in a bus
on the way to the Dead Sea.
'No, I like to,' I replied,
'but not at six in the morning.'
That evening I'd see him
throw a mattress round a garden
furiously, shouting
in his own language.
I'd stand and watch
for a quarter of an hour.

The young one was different,
always talking about a phone call
he was expecting.
He pummelled a punchbag
suspended from a tree
for one hour each afternoon
beneath a scorching sun.
And he'd run, for one hour,
then sit staring into space
while he got his breath back
for two hours.
The day they escorted the drunk one

onto the bus, making it clear
he'd better not come back,
the punchbag one forgot
to punch his bag.
Then remembered.

THE CHICKENS

Like a spiv
from the Second World War
he passes the chickens
through the dishwasher hatch,
turns and gets away quick
as I stuff them
in my laundry bag.

Two more hours
and the shift will be done.
I'll be in the shower,
then playing backgammon
in the afternoon sun.
The chickens defrosting.
None of us

can stomach
another kibbutz dinner –
cottage cheese, green peppers,
boiled eggs, stale bread.
The chickens down to me,
I'll sit back while the rest
do the work.

Tapping my feet
to the rhythm guitar.
The fire in the darkness,
our shapes huddled round it.
The meat sizzling, spitting.
The dogs inching closer,
told to lie down.

BRUISE

Since I slipped
and spent fifteen minutes
on my back moaning
at the hub of a circle
of concerned and amused faces
I've had pins and needles
in my right hand. I thought
I'd broken my elbow
but it was only bruised.
The doctor gave me some painkillers
which have a real buzz,
better than the vodka – 'wodka'
it says on the bottles here.
Actually, the wodka
tastes like petrol, not that

I've ever drunk petrol.
Listen, a few minutes ago
I put down Norman's book.
It was archetypal Norman,
I mean he was just
blowing his own trumpet,
and he doesn't even have
a very good one –
he must have bought it
at Woolworth's
back in the seventies.
'What was the book like?' Jeanette asks.
'It was interesting,' I reply,
'as was having a toe amputated
when I was nineteen.'

THE BARKING OF STRAY DOGS

The barking of stray dogs
outside my window
in the middle of the night
doesn't bother me
any more, not a bit,
well maybe a bit.
So much is funny
it's hard to know where to finish –
behaving like one
of the Blues Brothers,
or spending the whole day
slicing carrots, a man of my
whatever.

Tequila is good
mixed with grapefruit,
if you've the patience
to squeeze them. Traffic passes
and is not noticed,
like the early stages
of a mental illness.
The locals' word for a hangover
is also their word
for a stray dog.

POLITICS

It's like watching a film
of your own funeral.
You're shouting I'M ALIVE
but no one can hear you.

Across a room, two men
assess each other's silence.
They yawn and cough,
cross and uncross thin legs.

It takes years.
Ice forms on the cameras
that bring us news.
And then the men nod,

and then they rise.
One claps, then holds up a hoop
the other leaps through.
They both shout BOOM!

JUPITER

I've been lost in a study of Jupiter.
Thirty-three hundred times the size of earth

but no movie industry to speak of,
hence no awards ceremonies and no

microphones in the faces of nothing.
I explained all this in the town centre

but people seemed eager to ignore me.
Ah, people. They like to think they know me

by my black moustache and curly red wig
and the wheelchair I push in front of me

containing the rag doll, ukulele,
and the ghetto blaster I sing along with.

They know my favourite song is 'Love Me Do',
which I croon to a punk backing, they know

my coat for all weathers is grey cotton.
They don't know how I ache in these old bones.

They know yobbos sometimes gang up on me.
They don't know what the boots taste like.

RUM AND BLUE SKY

It was the time of day he liked the most,
before everyone got busy.
Just the one drink, straight down, then he was out,
striding along the disused railway track,
his old dog barely able to keep up.
All those people! He had no time for them,
them or their dull regulations.
He'd had no choice in jail, they'd seen to that;
that was part of it. Well he was free now.
He reached the bridge where he always turned back;
the sky was a clear blue pressed handkerchief.
He felt the weight of the bottle, kissed it,
took a mouthful of rum and kept going.

Through it all he stayed true to his own dreams.
And here he was, breathing. Even his dog
seemed to hear the promise the day whispered
to soar like a frisbee thrown at the sun.
He was humming something joyful, something
he couldn't put a name to but knew well.

I WAS AN UNARMED TEENAGER

Sunday morning, just after nine
or just before, and the Salvation Army band
strike up a dirge
right under the window.
I roll my hangover
from one red eye to the other, sit up
and stare down at the musicians
in their uniforms, rasping
their dirty hankie tune –
I shoot them
through their mouthpieces
with an imaginary gun.

My mother's getting warm
in front of an open oven,
a pot of tea just made,
Sunday People on the table
open at the crossword page,
and the dog slobbers toward me
with prisoner's eyes
but he's no chance
of a walk on the canal bank
right now. 'How do you die
like a cowboy,' my mother asks,
'four-three-four?'

COLD SPOT

I've taken to wearing
a jacket in the house,
it's colder than outside,
the walls are damp,
dripping sometimes,
this is a dump alright,
where I live, fastened in
with the noise of cars
and lorries streaming past,
in my head like harsh voices
or bad music, my breath
steaming up the window
as I stand watching
people without cars,
old, slow, cold, hanging on,
keeping death away
with whatever it takes
and their shopping bags.

I flush the toilet,
hear next door's baby
start to cry. I stand
and listen. It cries and
cries and cries.

SMOKE

The first time I lit up in front of him
it was about midnight,
I was watching The Marx Brothers with Dave.
I was fifteen, Dave was thirteen,
my dad must have been thirty-eight.
I was gagging for a No. 6,
willing my dad to fall asleep
in the chair like he often did.
I think the film was *Room Service*;
something they weren't at their best in.
I stared. I got more and more tense.
In the end I just lit a fag
like it was the most natural thing
in the world for me to do
and my dad
stood very slowly,
walked out and up the stairs
without a word
for months.

TWO LOVE POEMS

(i) Younger, Fresher

I got my hair cut
this morning, too short
is how it looks to me
but she likes it, Jeanette.
She says it makes me look
younger, fresher.
She says it makes me look
as if I know I'm living a life
that could be
much worse.
'Do you like them?' she asks,
turning her feet this way and that
in some new black
high-heeled sandals.

(ii) Bed Poem

She holds me from behind
or I curl up to her,
I like to feel her warm
backside. Like a workman's
brazier, I tell her.
Go to sleep, she murmurs.
I'm sure someone once said
a poem should be like an
onion, peeling it, layer after layer
bringing tears to the eyes,
but who'd want to wake up
in bed with that person?

SPLINTER
i.m. Mona Eileen Hattersley, 1935-1998

She said it was too small for her to see
and too small for my dad to see
but she had a splinter in her finger,

it was driving her up the wall –
this was when she was about fifty-five
so I was about thirty-four.

She passed me a pair of tweezers,
told me to take the splinter out
if I could see it. I could see it alright

and I got it with the tweezers
and pulled it straight out, no messing,
and my mother gave a sigh of relief.

Eight years later she was full of cancer,
drugged up, surrounded by cards and flowers,
fussed over by strangers in uniforms.

We took her home for the last month, she insisted.
'They can't make a proper cup of tea here,' she said,
'it's no wonder everybody's badly.'

AT THIS TABLE

I stare at the letter. It's from a young poet
who wants advice on how to get gigs in New York,
as if I could help him, barefoot and hungover

at this table in Huddersfield, up to my neck in shit.
This was meant to be my way out.
I'm laughing my head off the more I think of it.

I've been staying out of the sun, I get cold sores.
You have to avoid intimate oral contact,
where's the fun in that… Now Jeanette's telling me

about all the shopping trolleys in the canal
and on the bottom, plastic traffic cones.
The ducks appear unruffled however.

A TERRIBLE SONG

was just starting. I switched it off
and went to buy a loaf. I had the usual
small worries, sleeplessness
and being at the mercy of dentists,
fourteen hundred tons of job
and the chance I might drop dead
before crawling out from under it,
the possibility of reincarnation
as a business man's fat cigar,
forever puffed on, unlit in mean lips.
Like someone trying to escape through a porthole
getting their backside stuck, that's how
I felt, and that's not all, there was
a fresh bunch of flowers
tied to the bus stop down the street
again, a fresh bunch of flowers
is tied to the bus stop every Sunday.
I don't know why, I don't know
if I want to know. I don't know much
these days, but I do at least know
a terrible song when I hear one.

SMALL CHOCOLATE HEART

Estimated Cycle Time:
58.8 seconds

The press opens
I open the gate
remove the mould
I spray the tool
shut the gate
I push the green button
the press closes
I trim the mould
I pack the mould

Instructions To Operator:
Remove Feedgates Flush
Check Each Shot For
Pulling And Plucking

The press opens
I open the gate
remove the mould
I spray the tool
shut the gate
I push the green button
the press closes
I trim the mould
I pack the mould

It's ten in the morning
sunny and warm outside
I'm wearing tight shoes

The press opens

I open the gate
remove the mould
I spray the tool
shut the gate
I push the green button
the press closes
I trim the mould
I pack the mould

Remember: The Next Inspection
Is By The Customer

The press opens
I open the gate
remove the mould
I spray the tool
shut the gate
I push the green button
the press closes
I trim the mould
I pack the mould

Nine hours fifty-six minutes
four point eight seconds
to go

The press opens

THE DEPTH

Management. Two of them
and a couple of young lackeys
are in my way for half an hour
discussing the depth of the mould
coming out of the LB350
every 47.9 seconds.
'They won't wear it. I know
they won't.'
'But anything less and it would
fall off.'
I stop listening, try to carry on
as if they're not
present, as if I'm not,
as if I was under a parachute
gliding in a blue sky.
Then they are gone.
Our Quality Control Inspector
strides over.
'And what pearls of wisdom
did that lot have for you?'
They were talking, I tell him, about
the depth of the mould.
'The depth?' he says. '*The depth?*'
He turns, walks back to his office
shaking his head.
'They haven't got
a clue. Haven't got
a buggerin' clue.'

It's the sort of job where you lose
something, something
you spend the weekends
looking for with tired eyes.

POWDER MAN

'Fuck off!' he shouts.
'Get fucked!' I shout back.
It's how Jacko and I
say hello every day,
it keeps him happy
and amuses me too.
He's the powder man
who keeps the machines going,
it's a back-breaking job.
He prowls the factory
with a head full of films
like *Full Metal Jacket*,
punching things as he goes,
people if he's that way out.
In a US Marine haircut
he'll say, 'Outta the way, Buddy.'
His neck's thicker
than some girls' waists.
'I'd shag any woman,'
he informs me,
'except for one.'
He doesn't say
which one.

NO CHANCE

It's summer, and I stare
from where I'm stuck
trimming moulds for chocolate dog bones
across the floor at Ken,
who's fifty-seven,
who had a heart attack four years ago
during his dinner break.
There he is at the Fourteen Hundred,
hoisting hot, sharp, heavy fans,
sweat staining the back of his shirt
like a lake on a map, pouring down
his flushed forehead and face
and off the end of his nose.
He shakes his head and a thick spray
flies from his hair.
I can't watch too long, have to look away,
have to get on with my own work
which is just as tough
in this sort of heat.
I think if I had a heart attack
they wouldn't get me back in here
at gunpoint. That's obvious.
I wonder what Ken was scared of
and frown.

SUMMER SICK NOTE

We've got lavender toilet paper
made in Worksop
breakfast's on the go
I'm in the living room
watching the traffic
an endless procession
all sorts of vehicles
here on this road to Blackpool

a young black guy
in a red convertible
his shades reflecting
the bright morning sun
there goes someone with a canoe on their roof
another with a dog at the wheel
and one with a human head
stuck on the bonnet
it's going to be a hot day

my brother Dave is in Sweden
my great friend Nev, he's there as well
I'm not getting much done
but it beats the factory
beats it hands down
a bad case of the runs, I told them
it feels great to be here
with no clothes on

BAD ATTITUDE

We each took turns
to pick a cardboard box
up off the floor,
take three self-conscious steps
in slow motion
and put it down again,
and six months later
the Works Manager
gave us fancy certificates
saying we'd attended a course
in Manual Handling.
After I'd stopped laughing
the Works Manager told me
I'd a bad attitude;
he stood gaping
like I was something odd;
'but you turn up on time,'
he added, 'and do your job,'
and then he smiled
and I smiled
and he walked back to his office.

JOY

A young Sikh with a grin drives the taxi.
'I bet there's some joy and rejoicing
going on in there this Sunday morning,'
he says as we arrive. I laugh at that
and pay him and get out, moving
slowly, clock in and go to my machine
where the night shift operator
looks just about ready to climb the wall.
He's something of a smackhead, I've been told,
and I believe it, he's certainly weird.
But who on this planet isn't,
and aren't I working seven till seven
every Saturday and Sunday
and taking taxis to the stinking place?

I've dropped on for an easy job today
but stupidly have brought nothing to read
and have to scrounge round for something. I get
The Sunday Mirror, *The Sport on Sunday*
and Friday's *The Sun*, and I read all three
at great length, God help me, I read all three.

Y'KNOW WARRAMEAN?

Everything he tells you
he follows with the phrase
Y'know warramean?
He's used to drinking every night
Y'know warramean?
I don't mean he goes out every night
he might just have a few cans in the house
Y'know warramean?
If he could get out of the habit of drinking every night
then he wouldn't have to drink every night
Y'know warramean?
And you feel like grabbing hold of him and shouting
I'M NOT THREE YEARS OLD, OF COURSE I KNOW
WHAT YOU MEAN
Y'KNOW WARRAMEAN?
But you don't do that and he carries on
Y'know warramean?

He can't do overtime at the weekends
because of his Community Service
Y'know warramean?
He got done for almost nothing
well they called it assault
Y'know warramean?
I mean you can't call it assault
all he did was shout at her in the street
Y'know warramean?
Well she told the coppers he hit her
Y'know warramean?
Well he might have pushed her slightly
Y'know warramean?

It's ok, the Community Service
it'd be ok if you were getting paid
Y'know warramean?

BOSS ARSE

I almost got the sack,
I almost thumped a man
for the first time in twenty years,
a short fat strutting man
who thinks he knows who he is
and who I am, but who knows
less than corrugated cardboard
cut into strips, put in a pile,
less than rusty blades in a tin.
I can hardly believe he's real.
I could hardly believe him real
even as I shook my fist in his face –
'Fuck off you fucking little cunt!'
I should have been cooler somehow,
I should have been something like a freezer;
all afternoon I behave like someone
treading round a puddle of oil,
and the odious little man
still exists, scheming
in a brightly-lit office.

CHICKEN BONE CHARLIE

The three lads in the bus station
are just about legless, shouting 'Barmy Army'
over and over
as we wait for the
Marsden Hard End. It's 7.28
on a Saturday evening. I'm on my way home
from a grim job, not exactly enhanced
by the close company of Chicken Bone Charlie,
a scruffy-arsed little ragamuffin
who got on the wrong side of me
first thing in the morning
by playing a 90-minute Meat Loaf cassette
at full volume on his ghetto blaster.
We didn't speak from 7.15 a.m. to 6 p.m.,
despite working side by side. Then I said,
'Only one hour to go,' and he replied,
'Good. I'm sick of having to look at you.'
So I said, 'Even your best friend
must be sick of looking at *you*',
then neither of us
spoke again, as the last hour
dragged its heavy feet.

THE HANDSHAKE POEM

The summer's here, and the Managing Director
has just cleared out his desk, looking shaken
to be sacked for incompetence, and with rumours
of financial shenanigans and back-handers
laughed about openly on the shop-floor.

Last Christmas, he handed me a large box
of Cadbury's Milk Tray and said, glancing
at the name patch on my pale blue workshirt,
'Merry Christmas, Geoff', and shook hands with me
as though we were sealing a weapons deal.

And then, after catching me outside with a fag
when I should have been trimming lawnmower handles,
my first fag for three, nearly four long hours,
he gave me, some time in April or May,
my third written warning for misconduct.

The summer's here, and the Managing Director
has left the premises, his tail between his legs.
'They say he took ten grand from some Germans…'
We're all sure he's guilty, even if they prove him innocent.
Nothing could mar our ebullient mood.

I DID BRAIN SURGERY ON A BARNSLEY PUB FLOOR

Wayne by the juke-box
lost an eye at the weekend,
Wayne watching Wayne
and Wayne playing pool
broke both his arms –
he was complaining
he couldn't wipe his backside.

Wayne walked in
with a dog's skull in the palm of his hand –
'Alas, poor Wayne,
my fair sister,' he said.
He sat down at the bar,
in between Wayne
and Wayne.

Wayne proposed a toast
to Wayne,
but Wayne, Wayne and Wayne
refused to drink
and left in a bit of a huff.
'John Wayne films!
I bloody well can't stand them!'

shouted Wayne,
the uninjured one with the moustache.
I took my scalpel out,
introduced myself –
'Hello, I'm a surgeon
of some renown,
Dr. Wayne…'

HIS FINGERNAILS

I told him his hands were someone else's,
it was their fingernails he'd been chewing,
but he just laughed, as if I was joking.

So I pulled out a large brown envelope,
photographic evidence and so on,
dropped it on the table in front of him.

He stared at it and then he picked it up.
I tapped my feet and hummed 'Smokestack Lightning'
as he tried to take it all in, and then

he was sobbing and my arm was round him.
There, there, I said, you'll feel better later.
I was lying. He'd never feel better.

HE DREAMED HE BURST BALLOONS

He dreamed he burst balloons for a living
and was his own supervisor.
He worked twelve hours a week, made a good wage.

He was never exhausted, never bored.
He was calm like a cat full of tuna,
calm like a yacht in a sunlit harbour.

His past life had been forgotten
like a dull episode of a cop show.
There were no scars on his body.

SLEEPLESS

He woke just after one a.m.
to the familiar sound
of a police helicopter
circling over the mill, down the canal.
Naked in the darkness, he stood and watched.
Something seemed to be taking place
beneath the thick, dark trees.

The bastards had ruined his sleep.
He rolled a spliff, just a single-skinner,
some homegrown stuff, smoked it on the sofa
as the coppers hovered,
probing with their stupid spotlight
for any sign of life.

RED DUNGAREES
for TVR and Nichola

'Thank God,' she said, 'Friday, some music please,'
and she placed her bare feet on top of mine
beneath the table. She was somewhat hoarse

from shouting all day long, but a few drinks
soon put that right. I put 'Abbey Road' on,
it sounded great. George Harrison had died

the day before. 'I think I may have to
buy some new clothes,' I said, 'and stop smoking.'
They were two things I'd never said before

and her eyebrows went up. I lit a smoke.
'Know any shops that sell red dungarees?'
We sat there drunk and ha-ed and ho-ed and hee-ed.

P FOR POEM

I'm tired, slumped in a chair,
struggling to take it in –

aircraft crashing,
buildings collapsing,

dust and smoke and holy shit
everywhere.

Things can only get worse,
I mean better.

I can hear Death's Boots
shuffling on the Welcome mat –

'I don't need anything right now!'
I shout.

SOFA FACTORY

I was following a series
of red-lettered signposts:
SOFA FACTORY,
and an arrow, pointing.
I was wondering
if it said SOFA FACTORY
on every street-corner in town.
Then I came to a yard
with some huge iron gates
and above the gates in red paint:
SOFA FACTORY.

The job was dead easy.
All I had to do
was stick sofa catalogues
into envelopes,
put an address label on the front
and stamp them
second-class postage paid.
I kept looking at the clock.
I kept looking at it
like I couldn't believe it.

There were four of us
at a large table.
The others were young blacks.
One of them asked me
if I was an alky.
He said I had that look
about me.

The other two laughed
and I smiled and said
I couldn't afford to be an alky.
Which seemed to be an answer
everyone could live with.

SIXTEEN AT A TIME

I'm getting paid
minimum wage
to pack screws in plastic bags
sixteen at a time.
I'm working with a teenage girl
who's just had a ring
put in her eyebrow,
plays with it all the time.
She's what you'd call a chatterbox,
and always seems to be lurching
from one domestic crisis
to another. I get to hear
about her boyfriend, who has a steel plate
in his skull and sometimes
smashes the furniture – who once tried
to throw himself through
Burton's Menswear front window
but just bounced off,
went to sleep on the pavement.

Becky's ok, I like her. I told her
I was tired of having to listen
to Pulse radio, I wanted
Howlin' Wolf, Muddy Waters, Captain Beefheart –
'Whoever they're supposed to be!'
she said, laughing.
'People you've never heard of
might turn out to be the best people,'
I said. She said,
'How interesting.'
Then she asked if I wanted
a piece of her Yorkie
and I replied no thanks.

PRETTY FUNNY THINGS

It's hot in this hell-hole,
bastard roasting.
Half the women
sit in open blouses,
cleavage and patterned bras
and navel jewellery
all showing.

I've overheard some
pretty funny things,
like two eighteen-year-old girls
discussing cocksucking.
They had this conversation
in front of me in the canteen,
while I chewed my
cheese sandwiches and they
slurped chicken pot noodles.
To spit or to swallow,
that was the question.

Then there's Ugly Darren,
who brags about wanking
with his dirty socks round his cock.
One girl asked him
how many women he'd had sex with.
'Let me think… can you count
your sisters and your mam?'

THE NEXT BREAK

Working for this
tinpot agency.
They like me too
tired to think straight.
I spent eight hours today
folding paper in half
and sealing envelopes
in a large, cold room
with some other losers.
More than two hundred people
in rows of ten,
all of them
blathering
on and on,
or singing along
to the loud radios,
all the radios tuned
to the same crap station.
The sort of job
where all the time
you live only
for the next break,
the next chance
to stand outside smoking
in the freezing wind and rain.

STAND-IN

I'm standing-in
for a suicidal man,
doing his job.
It's boring, boring
like the life of a nail
in an old box.
I stand with folded arms
and yawn and watch
a circular saw
relentlessly spin,
stamping my boots
to keep my eyes open.

I wonder about him,
this man I've never met.
Everything I use
has his name on
in black felt pen
in capitals: LAWRENCE.
I know he's fifty-one,
off work with depression.
I know no one else here
likes him that much.
No one talks about him.
Asking gets me nowhere:
'Lawrence is Lawrence.'
That's all they'll give me.

STUPID STUFF

The supervisor
had something on his mind:
'Every time
you open a paper
there's some celebrity
showing their arse,
what's wrong
with these people?'
I thought about this
and other stupid stuff
as I toted heavy cardboard boxes
full of personnel files
up three flights of stairs.
Fifty-seven trips
on one of the hottest
days of the year.
Tom said he'd report me
to the union
for sweating on the job.
But we don't have a union.
Then we heard on the radio
that Dennis Thatcher
had passed on.
Shirley said, 'Poor Maggie',
and I laughed.
But to her it was no joke.
Funny how you can
go off people.
Well, I'm sure she's gone off
me too.

SMALL MAN IN A SMALL TOWN

The supervisor
had something on his mind:
'The world would be
a better place
if we killed ten pakis
every morning.'
My God, you have to put up
with some shit
if you want to keep a job
nowadays.
Fifteen minutes later
he's back, telling me
asylum seekers
should be castrated
so they can't fuck
any English women.
I'm not kidding,
I have to listen to this
every day
from seven thirty till five,
when I make my dash for
freedom.
I stand at the bus stop
smoking
as stones clatter
the roof of the shelter
thrown by kids
from a bridge
over the road.
Nice kids
with nice dads
with love
in their hearts.

THAT WAS YOUR LIFE

I can't believe how fast
it all goes by,

seven years from now I'll be sitting round
and I'll be fifty-three.

Sixteen years from now I'll be sitting round
and I'll be sixty-two.

Twenty years ago I was sitting round
and I was twenty-six.

ALL WEEKEND

He tried to ignore it.
He took all his clothes off,
slumped down at the kitchen table.
He smoked a lot, coughing a lot.

He paced about the room.
He stood at the window, stared out.
'I can't stand it!' he said aloud,
but he knew he'd have to.

UNDER STRICT ORDERS

She banned him from the living room
at her thirteenth birthday party.
She was sure he'd embarrass her
in front of all her friends.
She told him straight: she was growing up.
He was no longer required
to play the fool, blow balloons up
or supervise pass the parcel.
He was a prehistoric fart
best left alone in the kitchen
with his bottles of wine
and personal stereo.

He was whistling
'Mr Tambourine Man'
when she burst in
and told him to shut up.
He came that close
to embarrassing her.

CHICKEN CASHEW NUTS

There's a full moon tonight
over Salendine Nook
as he looks out licking his lips.
They took more than two hours
to deliver the meal
three quarters of a mile.
His fortune cookie says
there is a lot of stuff
he wants out of his life,
stuff like desks, swivel chairs
and prats sitting in them.

Suddenly he comes round
in a roomful of aliens
from the planet Solemn.
Luckily he's wearing
his brand new silver-grey
attitude coat.

MAN ENDURING HEATWAVE

He's sitting there
wearing nothing
but underpants.

He's only wearing those
because
he's no curtains.

*

He's come up with a list –
ten things he needs to start doing.
That's a load off his mind.

He feels like getting drunk, celebrating.
In fact he already did, yesterday.
But he feels like celebrating again.

*

He's way deep into
John Coltrane's
A Love Supreme –

finds it hard to believe
Coltrane's favourite dish
was fried brains.

UNSHAVEN POEM

God save us from the professors.
They're a hard to please bunch alright.
All they need do is open the packet
and they're the world's biggest experts.
There's a kind of night

when all I'm good for
is connecting with the world wide cobweb
to take on other fools at backgammon.
It's a sad way to go, I need slapping.
I'll be growing a beard if I'm not careful.

STOCKINGS AND SLIPPERS

Jeanette's hanging
stockings
out on the line.

I watch
from the kitchen
with her sister.

She won't wear them
herself, she says,
stockings,

she just can't get
on with
suspender belts.

I say I need
a new pair of
slippers;

it's no joke,
I need them,
I'm serious.

Then Jeanette's back:
'That's that
bloody job done.'

WORKING THROUGH

Once they got going
the band weren't too bad
for a bunch of old drunks,
I was there till
after midnight.
I hardly slept at all
and the next day
on the machine
was living hell.
It was one of
the hottest days
of the year
and one of
the hardest jobs
I'd had.
I started out
at seven a.m.
thinking
I'd never
make it.
But like a nail
working through
an old shoe
it slowly
turned into
seven
p.m.
and I was still
breathing
and I still knew
who I was.

WHEN YOU'RE PUSHING FIFTY

When you're pushing fifty
it gets harder to wake
to shake off the drink
shave with a clear head
get out in time for the bus
do a hard day's labour
the sweat pouring out of you
with a bitter smell

When you're pushing fifty
you've dreamt most of your dreams
can't recall them now
all that remains
are the motions you go through
saying the same things
as if you still meant them
through what's left of your teeth

When you're pushing fifty
you've read all the great books
know there are none to come
you don't believe in miracles
you no longer hope
for social change
know phonies and killers
will always be in charge

When you're pushing fifty
you've suffered a lot of fools
now you show them the door

you just follow your own nose
it's smelled most stuff by now
it knows bullshit for instance
it can smell a rat
or a rare flower

When you're pushing fifty
you know you don't know everything
you know enough
you know just as much as you can take
you know a good move when you see it
or a bad mistake
there's a lid on your rage
now and then you hear it hissing

SCOTCHING THE SEAGULL RUMOUR

It was a gaggle of geese
that chased us off the beach,
who'd be scared of seagulls?
Twenty-five geese though
all running at you
wings outstretched,
that's an amazing sight.
And the noise they made!

Later we took a cruise
on a paddle steamer
down the River Clyde,
saw dolphins alongside
leaping out of the water
just like in the movies.

MOOSE FACE, WOBBLE AND PLONK

Michael Bruce got voted Chest Of The Year
by the readers of *Smash Hits* in '71,
but Yvonne Plonk revealed she fancied me
because I resembled one of The Sweet,
especially my mouth shared the shape of his.
This information made me feel quite sick –
only now can I speak of it lightly,
three hundred thousand cigarettes later.

The other girls who courted me back then
were Moose Face and Wobble, neither of whom
made me feel like dancing. Their name for me
was Mad Geoff. They had this running joke –
if you're going to have one sore tit
you might as well have two. It was over my head,
as were so many things. I was posing like mad
and this took up most of my energy.

LOOKING HARD, FEELING MEAN

Ben shouted down to come on up.
I was in the middle of the living room floor,
playing air guitar to 'School's Out'.
A pall of smoke hung in the air,
empty cans of Skol were scattered around.
The song finished, 'Looney Tune' started up,
I walked to the foot of the stairs,
up the stairs. There was no light at all,
four closed doors. Where are you? I shouted.
A bedroom door opened and there they were,
Ben and Roy, no clothes on, full erections.
Roy's cock was huge, Ben's puny next to it.
Ben got hold of Roy's cock, yanking it up and down.
They were both laughing, I stood there watching
then I turned round, went back downstairs,
sat on the sofa, lit a cigarette,
found a can of Skol with a bit still in,
listened to the rest of Side One, stood up
and took the record off, put it back in its sleeve,
the famous sleeve in the shape of a desk
with a pair of knickers inside.
I held the album in my right hand
and left the house, walked home
through streets full of sunlight, full of
women and pushchairs and babies, old men,
walked home realising my best two friends
weren't people I thought I ever wanted
to set eyes on again.

DON'T LEAN ON THE SIDEBOARD

I was always accused by Grace
of stopping her clock
by leaning on the sideboard –
'Don't lean on the sideboard
you'll stop the clock!'
became a catchphrase among my cronies,
something someone would come out with
at a boring football match or
brooding as we walked home
from the school dance.

The very first time I got drunk,
I mean so drunk I couldn't stand,
I said it to the doctor who examined me
in the Emergency Department
of Barnsley General Hospital –
'Don't lean on the sideboard
you'll stop the clock!'
I slurred, laughing
like it was the funniest thing
anybody had ever said.

SUNRISE

Sunrise –
a fat man
running from his bed
wearing only a vest
is a much less
beautiful sight,
as is a cat
eating a moth,
as is an ashtray
full of death.
Things can get funny
when you've had no sleep
as if they weren't
funny already.
A long way off
maybe a dog will bark,
my chest will wheeze
like a faulty machine
and a number of wasps
will be trying to get
in here.

Nobody said
they wanted this
war all the time,
they weren't asked.
The world's full of
empty stomachs,
they'll have to stay like that.
Family viewing's
making a comeback.

Outside the Blue Hebium

Smith/Doorstop, 2012

IN THE ROOM AND OUT THE DOOR

He likes this room. It's where he is
when all he does is what he wants

and only hears voices
he wants to hear. Now and then

he steps outside, sniffs the rain,
stands and stares with a slight grin

at the disagreeable scene.
He shivers, goes back in

to the woman he loves.
Right now she's painting –

she does watercolours, landscapes.
He can only sketch a matchstick man

kneeling in front of a matchstick woman,
and he places this on her easel,

making her laugh, turn and kiss him
all in one swift movement.

He'd hate to be with a woman
and it not mean anything,

like she was an old work shirt
and he no longer worked.

SNAPPED

I snapped my feet
as I got out of bed.
Then I thought I'd better
snap them again, individually.

Snapped the curtains, then opened them.
Saw a cat on a car roof – great snap!

I snapped the kettle
after I'd filled it,
then again after I'd switched it on
with the red light showing.
Got it a third time,
steam pouring out.

Snapped my tea with the steam rising.
Snapped it after it had cooled down.

Snapped my face in the mirror
before shaving, twice during, and after.
Snapped myself brushing my teeth,
it wasn't easy.

Snapped a blue fly, two times:
alive on a chopping board,
dead on a chopping board.
Snapped a beer can
floating down a river
at the back of my mind.

The phone rang, I snapped it.
Didn't take the call.
Then at last I sat down
to edit the past thirty minutes.

TEN HEBIUMS
for Edith Smits

1.

Women are wired up
in the hebium,
babbling into face attachments,
their efficiency closely monitored –
no birthday cards or greetings here,
no wild weekends dissected,
no time even for an air kiss.
Women have long legs
in the hebium,
watch out you don't trip over them.

2.

He was hoping to have hebium.
He was trying to have hebium.

He thought of how other people had hebium.
People had a limitless capacity for hebium,

everywhere he looked people were having hebium.
So why wasn't he having any hebium?

He recalled ways he'd had hebium.
Ho ho, but none seemed, now, like hebium.

What kind of a concept was hebium
anyway? Serious people don't care about hebium.

Nothing happened, then it happened again.

3.

He'd penned, he said, so far this year,
approximately two thousand hebiums.
Not bad going for May the seventeenth.

Apparently, he's had hebiums published
all over the place, and Cheesy Rupert
kept nine for further consideration.

4.

I've just given us both
permission to get drunk.

'Henry', I said, 'it's time
to get blotto'.

So I talk to the hebium, so what?
It's not as if I expect a reply.

5.

We shared a bottle of hebium;
I dreamt my wife was groped
by the harmonica player
in an all-girl blues band
and that a cheese sandwich
almost broke my neck;
soon it was morning, but what morning?

6.

She's pouring Earl Grey tea
from a silver pot
that catches the sun;
he can see her hebium

as she hums a soft tune
that floats on the breeze
of another day
that was only dreamt up.

7.
Sometimes
whole days
go by

without
him once
hiding

inside
the blue
hebium.

8.
Happy Hebium, Honey!

9.
'Infection of the hebium', he said.
I'd rather have heard anything but this.
He said, 'You've a hebium infection',
as if it was nothing to fret about,
as if nothing was what I was.

10.
When you whisper my name
I feel like Bogart in his prime.

I don't have a hebium to die for
and that suits me just fine.

INFAMOUS

His life had been ruined by a misprint.
While still only fifteen, he embarked upon

a steamy love affair with a manure woman.
It was all so unfair, he'd been doing alright.

He felt stupider than a football team,
stupider than an army or a government.

'At this moment in time, I wish I was dead',
he said. I said, 'I wish you were dead too'.

YOU DON'T DREAM AT ALL IF YOU CAN HELP IT

It's tough for a spoilt kid in a cold world
and you're grateful you were never that kid

but still the world is tough, the world is tough.
Banks and charities and castles and locks –

stuff that makes no sense everywhere you look.
You feel like you've been to the moon and back

only for some nitwits to convince folk
you were fooling around in a desert.

If you're lucky you'll make it to sixty,
you already like playing the old man.

You try hard not to think of the future,
a place where kids play games with human bones.

GOOD DAY IN THE LAB

We put the finishing touches
to our cure for hiccups – the answer

lay in torturing baby koalas
slowly to death, who'd have thought it.

We wiped a clear spot on the big window,
looked outside for the first time in ages.

PARTY PEOPLE

He felt quite out of things
without an abdominal scar
to show everyone

but then he remembered
he was the only one
with an amputation.

DEAR FRIEND

It's been a while, I know, forgive me please.
Things have been like a movie no one likes,
then I saw a young kestrel clinging to a wall,
wings spread out like a giant brown butterfly.
Its head turned round as it returned my gaze.

Dear friend, I wish I could get good money
to show a few film clips and talk nonsense
but I'm not a chosen one, just a loon.
I used to fight soldiers for fun.
I'm still nothing like a people person.

Dear friend, there goes another foul
slobbering brute on the end of a lead.
He's got a dog with him as well. Sometimes
I think I must have missed the big event
because the subtitles were off that day.

Dear friend, the sun goes down and I wake up.
I have a bottle and another bottle and
lots more bottles, and our dear friend Shaky.
He's a drinking man and a smoking man.
There are less and less of us left.

THE CONFRONTATION

'You've got baked beans and peas,
what do yer need greens for?'
I turn and catch a pale slits-for-eyes face
beneath the rim of a blue baseball cap.
'What're you lookin' at?' he spits.
His wife is about fourteen inches tall.
This takes place somewhere
near Woolworth's, somewhere
near life gone cold or death warmed up.
Couple number something billion something
in the contest of life.
'One minute you've got a precious guitar', I say,
'the next you've got a pile of wood'.
'Yer what', he whines, 'say that again, I dare yer'.
I say, 'One minute you've got a bedroom window,
the next you've got a headless cat'.

RUMP POEM

She's got to be eighty,
blotto in a ratty fur coat,
swigging house red
while he clings to a pint of something dark.

No they don't mind if I join them.
She's Elisabeth and he's Ron.
Ron is her third husband, she says –
'I think I preferred my second,
both to this one and to the first'.

Her second husband died –
accidentally suffocated
beneath her bare buttocks
when she became engrossed
in the collected works
of Edgar Allen Poe.
Remarkable enough,
but husband number one
had perished the same way.

Husband the Third pipes up:
'Your friend is right, sheep cough,
I've heard them cough myself, and cows'.
He starts to shake and drops his glass,
which still held one good slurp.

'Now you see what I've got to put up with',
comments Mrs Buttocks,
looking at me as if I had
f o u r on my forehead.

HIS FAULT

It was his fault the window broke
because he ducked
when I threw the hammer

and it was his fault the dog died
because he left it
with me.

It was his fault the house burned down
because he knew
I had an issue with matches

and he had a box of Swan Vestas
on the side
in plain view.

POEM FOR KYLIE

She had long hair,
one of the shits had hold of it,
dragged her round by it
while the other two took turns
to boot her in the face.
I started shouting
from my fourth floor window
leave her alone, I'm calling the police,
leave her alone.
Then she was flat out in the road
and they were walking off
but one turned back, started stamping
on her head like a loon
and I ran straight down there
in my bare feet.

She was moaning, trying to move.
There were teeth on the ground –
blood all over the place.
Her hair was thick with blood.
She kept spitting
mouthfuls of blood.
Her cheekbones were broken
or her eye sockets.
I could hardly believe
she was conscious.
She was such a small girl,
five feet, maybe, six stone.
She could just about speak,

told me she was eighteen
and her name was Kylie.
I held her in my arms
till the ambulance came.
It took more than an hour.

There are these times
when all I can do
is sit in the dark
listening to music.
I've got thousands of songs
by hundreds of singers.
All the singers are dead
or soon will be.

IMPIOUS

There's nothing pleasant
inside a church or
outside one either,
you can get the shakes
just walking past.

'Morning', says a man
who wants you to live
to be a hundred
and seven and not
enjoy one minute.

FORTUNE COOKIE

Soon you'll quit the bottle,
get religion, and fall in love
with a new bank account.

You'll be able to fill
a stadium with enemies,
a phone box with real pals.

You'll have a toe chopped off;
you'll spend less time cutting your nails.
You'll kick up quite a fuss.

You'll meet a man who's thinking of
becoming a poet.
He'll say this quite seriously.

THERE'S NOT MUCH FISH IN A FISH PIE IS THERE

There are folk who don't know how to pay bills.
How long before we shoot them in kindness?

You think of this stuff as you get older
when there's not even a whiff of success.

The train ride's a week's wage, so get walking.
Twelve miles a day never killed anyone.

Tread through the crumbling decay and learn it.
Everyone here gets an education.

YE MERRY GENTLEMEN

They kicked us out at three in the morning,
a great crowd of drunkards
finding ourselves
in the middle of a heavy snowfall
which instantly became
a snowball fight.

It began with everybody laughing
but soon grew too vicious
to be called fun.
Weaklings were bombarded mercilessly,
and when one man slipped down
our boots went in.

I woke to find the toes on my right foot
were black and blue
and limped and hopped down stairs
to stand on the doorstep, smoking, yawning,
croaking 'Happy New Year'
at all who passed.

NINETEEN EIGHTY-FOUR

There were policemen and
police vans and
police dogs and
police horses
all over
South Yorkshire.

You met an anarchist
who'd spent eight years in jail.
He was a good man.
He liked Captain Beefheart
and the Bonzo Dog Band.
He had a load of hash
buried in his garden
and he dug up three ounce,
sold it to you at a very
nice price.

BERNARD'S

Like a small cinema in a pig sty
with a fat man in the centre
rolling fat joints, breathing noisily.
The fire's blazing, he's in an open robe,
belly ahead of him like a buffer,
pendulous breasts covered in ginger hairs.

There are piles of magazines and papers,
chocolate wrappers, coke cans, pizza boxes.
There's a heap of bones on a greasy tray
among the ashtrays and paraphernalia.
Sixteen, all gnawed as if by a starved dog.
There's mould on the carpet between his slippers.

It's not long before he's red in the face,
shouting and shaking his flabby fist
at the brand new fifty-four inch HDTV.
'*The BB bastard C! Multicultural scum!*'
He'll calm down long enough to smoke a joint
and open a packet of custard creams.
Then he'll be off again, spitting crumbs.

He's never held a job more than two days.
Now he claims there's something wrong with his neck.
He winds you up with every word he says
but lacks the courage of his convictions:
there's a racist poster in his window;
it comes down when he phones for a curry.

NO ONE KNOWS WHY

Old dogs in the garden, barking
Barking all night, into morning

Turning slightly in a cool breeze
A man on the end of a rope

Barking all night, into morning
Turning slightly in a cool breeze

Calmly tied the rope to a beam
Had to get something right for once

Last fish 'n' chips supper, the final cigarette
Snapshots spread out on the table

Had to get something right for once
Calmly tied the rope to a beam

He jumped through the trap door
Meant to smile but he sobbed

Snapshots spread out on the table
Last fish 'n' chips supper, the final cigarette

He jumped through the trap door
A man on the end of a rope

Meant to smile but he sobbed
Old dogs in the garden, barking

THE GAME

The object of the game
is to punish yourself,
those who love you,
and everybody else.

All you're ever paid
are thanks or no thanks,
usually no thanks
or not even that.

It's a glorious game
make no mistake,
one day you'll be glad
for thanks or no thanks.

ALIVE NOT DEAD

1. Sober
He stopped
drinking

three days
ago.

It seems
longer.

2. The Night
A plate on the table,
crumbs on the plate.

He sits and stares
at the crumbs and the plate.

He rolls another smoke
just for something to do.

Then he smokes it
without thinking.

3. Test Results
It was so good to learn from his doctor
that he wasn't dying –
he felt like cart-wheeling across her desk
and kissing her, although
she reckons his beer belly is grotesque,
that he should be ashamed.

TIN BATH AND SCARY HOLE

In 1969 I was thirteen
and in the mornings as I got ready for school
Radio One would be playing
and one of the few things I was sure of
was that I didn't want to grow up
to be anything like Tony Blackburn.
Our house had no bathroom,
just an outside toilet,
which made for a tin bath
in front of the fire once a week
and a cold seat over a scary hole
at the bottom of a dark yard.
I was starting to take
an interest in girls,
but I didn't know any
apart from those who lived on my street
and they weren't the ones
I was becoming interested in.

In 1969 the USA
landed on the moon
or pretended to
and some stoned overgrown kids
believed themselves stardust
as they wallowed in mud.

FATTY FAIRHOLME'S GANG

A young gang of rockers
in denim and leather
gathered every evening
in front of the town clock,
getting in people's way,
trying hard to look hard.
They owned one motorbike,
and every now and then
one of them would jump on,
kick it into life and roar off
down Station Road – about
a hundred yards and then
a death-defying turn
to avoid the working men's club.
Sometimes two or three or
even four would be on the bike,
laughing and shrieking like children,
and one night they tried it with nine.

We heard the bang clearly
over the noise of the telly
and rushed outside; other houses
were emptying, someone shouted,
'Fatty Fairholme's been in a crash!'
We ran to the end of the street -
rockers lay sprawled all over.
Miners spilled out from the club,
stood round with pints and fags
to wait for the ambulances.
There were some broken limbs,

lots of blood from busted noses,
but no one was dying.
'I'll kill that bastard wall',
mumbled Fatty Fairholme.
Everybody agreed
it served the silly buggers right.

BREATHLESS

Struggling on the corner
to find his breath, the old miner
looks up to see the sun
break through black clouds, shine straight
into the doorway of the Prince
where now he spots a girl
smoking behind a grin
that all but breaks his spirit –
she's laughing at him
as he leans with one hand
on the edge of Phil's Butcher's
wheezing and hoicking phlegm.
Used up, with white whiskers.
Phil steps out in a bloody apron:
'Eyup owld lad are tha alreyt?
Tha not 'elpin' mi custom much tha knows.'

TWO BOYS, THREE FISH, AND ONE DAD

It meant nothing to me
but I was persuaded
to go with my friend Glyn
on a fishing trip
off the coast of Cleethorpes.
We went out on a boat
with about twenty other fools,
got wet through and frozen;
somehow I caught three fish
but all Glyn ended up with
was a red nose.

His dad was supposed to meet us
afterwards on the pier.
When we spotted him
approaching through the crowd
I handed Glyn one of my fish,
the biggest. Glyn said nothing
and we stood there solemnly
as his dad walked up to us.
'I see Geoff caught the most',
he said, laughing.
'Yes', I said, 'but Glyn
got the biggest one'.

Glyn and I were good friends then,
had been all our lives,
but it changed completely
when we were sixteen or seventeen.
There was no big falling-out;

all of a sudden, we couldn't talk
any more, we seemed
to have nothing in common.
I haven't spoken to him
or set eyes on him
for more than thirty years.

AFTER THE STUPID FILM

When the film was over,
after what seemed a very long time,

he went into the next room
where his wife was painting,

bent over and asked her
to give him a good kick.

She refused, of course.
'And I thought you loved me', he said.

His wife remained intent
on her spooky landscape,

but smiled at the edge of her lips.
As he stared over her shoulder,

splashes of red and silver
leapt out at him like shrieks.

He said, in his famous
impression of Neil Young,

'Kinda innarestin.'
On a patch of bare ground

lit by a full moon,
many things were dying.

Instead of an Alibi

Broken Sleep Books, 2023

New Thing

NEW THING

It came out of thin air, out of nowhere.
Once it was here, no one could imagine
how the days had gone by before, to what purpose.

Old habits die hard was found to be wrong.
New Thing was what no one could avert their gaze from.
Rockets were fired; fortunes were made, lost, and made again.

One little girl drew a picture of it that won a prize.
A guitarist composed a symphony, got an award.
No one saw the picture, nor heard the symphony,

they were too busy with it, the new thing.
New Thing seduced people, collected them.
It knew it would always be the new thing.

MOTIONS

Like placing a sticking plaster
over a shotgun wound,
we're all wasting our time

with these green bins,
but it keeps some folk happy
to go through the motions.

Here's my contribution,
which includes poetry
to give the bin some soul,

the work of years or
the play of years,
the work and the play being the same thing.

STUCK WITH IT

He looks like he ended up with the face he earned
after smoking opium for ten years
through the oily barrel of a rifle.

There's a whole bunch of thugs riding his bones.
Trying to make sense of it all has worn him down.
Right place, wrong time, no luck, no hope, nothing.

Reckless, stupid, heading for the nearest
meathead magnet, size ten steel toe capped boots
stamping out a stupid, reckless rhythm.

There's an old jazz melody in his head.
Orange was the colour of her dress, then blue silk.
It's good to think of stuff like that at times like this.

EXPECTING TO BE HOMELESS

Looks to me like it's got more snow in it.
That's what he says, peering seriously at the sky.
He stands in six inches of snow and peers.

This new weather won't be much fun when we're homeless.
Let's chill out and listen to Charles Mingus.
I speak his name through what's left of my teeth.

He stands in six inches of snow and peers.
I'll tell thee what, he says, we'll have a drink.
We sit freezing, supping cider, quiet.

There are folk who wish they were dead, but we're not them.
Let's chill out and listen to Mr Ellington.
I speak his name with what's left of my breath.

STRAIGHT, NO CHASER

What they call a disposable income –
he's not really got one

right now, just a list of things he covets,
like the complete works of Thelonious Monk

on pristine vinyl, and a tin of beans.
Only joking! He's got a tin of beans,

got two. In the cupboard. Next to the peas.
On the shelf between the two empty shelves.

No end to the insults, no end to them.
Don't you worry about me, pal,

I can live on ten pence a bastard day.
And still have something left over.

INSTEAD OF AN ALIBI

He needs an alibi
for every single day of the past forty years
and he's struggling, struggling.

He lights his pipe, inhales –
holds the smoke in till his fat face looks sure to burst
and does, with an encore.

Flicking through his first collection
he's surprised by a decent poem,
tucked away on page 56

like a best pair of shoes
in the bottom of a wardrobe
that's going up in flames.

GRUMPY

The train's packed, standing room only.
Everyone's eyes are down, staring dully

into small electronic screens,
their thumbs like pale, agitated creatures –

God's second son
could fly by the window on a winged pig

and not one of them would notice,
not one.

I met someone who could still concentrate
on just one thing for more than one minute,

then I found gold
in the streets of Milnsbridge.

ACTION

One time I was a computer salesman
who stapled his scrotum to his thigh for a bet
and that wasn't even the stupid bit.

Next thing I was the world's least competent vet.
I got mauled by a lion but survived
long enough to ask for a glass of milk.

I died, often grimly, most of the time.
Strictly bit parts, year after year, shot after shot.
You'll have seen me somewhere, with my sour face.

Now I've been reinvented as a ruthless thug.
The end of the world is round the corner
and everyone has to pay up on time.

AFTER

Seven a.m., the sun already ferocious.
Poking through the remains of last night's barbecue –
someone's guard dog, very tasty.

We banged an old book on the fire -
a man who reads was stoned to death
the other night. No one likes a reader.

I find a pile of pigeons' feet by the cesspit,
hundreds of them. Feathers floating about.
Whoever did it owns a nifty blade.

The search for clean water goes on.
It's the Government's last initiative. I may sign up -
you get an egg and fresh bread every day.

MASTER OF CEREMONIES

What tripe some of them come out with.
There's one who wants to be introduced as
the finest love poet of his generation –
seems to expect me to keep a straight face -
and a fat git who aims to outdrink Bukowski,
and at one point will sing a rousing sea shanty.

When young Murphy's blotto cousin
falls off his stool, flat on his face
halfway through a solemn piece
about kissing and touching,
I laugh like mad, the whole room
laughs like mad.
The finest love poet isn't impressed –
tells me off later, the surly fucker.

Next month we have five poets for the price of four.
Thank you all for coming tonight, I hope you enjoyed it.
Thanks especially to the poets themselves.
Let's have one more round of applause.

HEMINGWAY IN 10 TRUE SENTENCES

At the age of eighteen he was blown up
while eating a cheese sandwich.

Sheltering in warm cafes in Paris
he came up with some of his best stories.

After Paris he did the one bad thing
for which he could never forgive himself.

He'd kill a deer, or a brown bear, or a lion
without a second thought.

He'd pick a fight with anyone
if he was sure he could beat them.

He survived two plane crashes in two days
but he wasn't unhurt.

His hair and bushy beard went white
but he didn't look like Father Christmas.

Winning the Nobel Prize for Literature
failed to cheer him up.

He stabbed old friends in the back with a smirk;
electric shock treatments all but finished him off.

Mary found what was left of his head
dripping from the ceiling and walls.

WHAT I'M UP TO

Buying a washing machine,
that's what I'm up to.

I've checked out the website
but you really need to see a washer

in the flesh, so to speak.
And here they are - hundreds

of freestanding washing machines,
row upon row, two levels –

washers as far as the eye can –
maybe not hundreds, let's be fair.

They all look the same to me
but the prices vary. I stand and stare at them

like a stuffed cat. My head fills with figures -
load capacity, spin speed, other stuff.

Here comes a salesperson, at last,
a sullen young Asian, face like thunder.

'Can I help you?' he barks.
Must have had a worse night than me.

KNIFE

Always carry a knife
in case he starts on you,
folk have stabbed him before,
it usually stops him.

Not quite what I wanted
or expected to hear,
my first day on the job,
about to meet the boss.

WAITING FOR IT TO DIE

He phoned the RSPCA.
They said they'd be eight hours, eight hours at least.
That's great, he thought, just bloody great.
He sat close to the dog on the bloody carpet.

It was conscious, its eyes followed his every move
while its body remained completely still
as a dark pool formed beneath it and spread.
It had hopped in through the open front door and dropped.

Time dragged. A headache hit him hard
as the dog yelped wildly, then fell quiet again.
There was barely any flesh left on its front legs,
just streams of blood down twisted bones.

It was a black and white dog, about three years old.
If he moved his hand toward it, it growled.
The name on its collar was Benjamin.
He sat and watched its eyes lose their sparkle.

ARTHUR'S IN GRIMSBY

He's getting worried
about the weekend –
Arthur's in Grimsby,
Albert's in Thailand.
He could end up
staring at the floor drunk.

He could end up
sitting at a table
eating something
so unhealthy it would scare him
if only he was that little bit
more alert.

He could end up
stuck with someone
who shoots rabbits for fun,
who'll tell him, dead normal,
his ambition's to be an
assassin.

He could end up
with a pile of paper
in front of him,
paper with words on, like
mongoose, tyrant, claptrap,
pedestrian.

HEAD OF STEAM

He's the ugliest gravedigger
in the whole of England,
that's his boast anyway,
a well-battered skinhead
growing more dangerous
and stupid with each drink,
a nutcase who could change
your life in an instant.
I'll have to think before
I speak, think twice;
he's already threatened
to smack my face in once,
when I said I didn't care
whether or not Janeway
was a better captain
than Picard and Kirk.

IN T' GEORGE

1. *Stan and His Lass*

Ah've lost mi bastard coyt ageeun
Ah'm allus loyzin' it
In pubs, tha knows, pissed up
Tek it off 'n' forget

Ar lass reckons ah'm mental like
That's a laugh comin' from 'er
Some o' t' stunts shiz pulled o'er t' years
Mad cow!

That time shi come in t' pub
'n' put mi Sunday dinner o'er t' top o' mi 'eeud!
The' we' mashed taties darn t' back o' mi collar
The' we' carrots 'n' sprouts 'n' all soorts

Tha knows what shi reckons meks a good breakfast?
A bleedin' apple
That's all, nowt else, just a bleedin' apple
A bleedin' apple on a bleedin' little plate

2. *Don's Watter*

Ah remember when ah wa' a young 'un
Ah biked it to 'arrogate
All t' way, non-stop, in t' bloody sun
Abart eleven ah wa'

Ah were deein' o' thust
Ah knocked on a dooer
'n' asked for a drink o' watter
Did ah gerra drink? Did ah 'eck

Ah'll tell thee summat
Tha'd 'ave ter knock
On a lorra bloody dooers in Wombwell
Afore tha farnd someb'dy

That wun't gi' a kid
A drink o' watter
Tha'd 'ave ter knock
On a lorra bloody dooers all reyt

3. *Sam's Absence from the Horse Shoe Explained*

Ah remember walkin' art o' t' 'oss shoe
This is abart thirty years sin'
Ring Mi Bell wa' on t' juke box
Remember that shite?

Suddenly ah guh flyin'
Ah'm darn on t' floor 'n' ah look up
There's these three lasses in jeans 'n' leather
Stood sneerin' darn at mi

Ah tell thee, ah gorrup 'n' walked art
'n' ah nivver went back ageeun
Ah thought, well, that's enough fer me
If even t' lasses're lookin' fer a feyt nar

It shook mi up a bit ah'll tell thi
It's not like the' w're lads
Wunt raise an eyebrow these days would it?
'n' they'd put t' boot in 'n' all

4. *Cockroach's Lament*

When ar wa' a young 'un
Resin wa' better 'n' grass
Tha on'y smoouked grass
If tha cun't get nowt else

Tha can't even buy resin ner moor
Not that's any good any rooud
'n' that skunk stuff, ah dun't know
Ah can't be doin' wi' it

Ah'd love a good smoke o' resin though
Afghan black, summat like that
Like it used ter bi, ah meeun, back in t' days
Tha cun't g' wrong wi' that stuff

Thi mind went fuckin' ivvrywheeur
It wa' like all 'n a sudden tha understood stuff
This skunk's nowt like that
Just meks thi even moor mental than tha are already

5. *Fat Al Dismisses Pig Parker's Literary Ambitions Out of Hand*

Iz started writin' stuff tha knows
'ad a couple o' stories in this magazeeun
'e showed it mi, di'n't look like much ter me
But tha'd a thought 'e'd won t' Nobel prize 'r summat

Nar, like, 'e's all lardy da
Dun't even talk ter nob'dy ner moor
Thinks 'e's gunner bi a gret writer
Ah'm not bleedin' jokin'

Ah tell thi, me 'n' thee, wiv got moor chance
O' bein' t' next men on mooin
Gret writer f' fuck's sake!
Livin' in a world o' 'is ooun

Can tha imagine anybody comin' back from t' shop
Carrying a book written by yon?
Ah allus thought 'e wa' a bit 'n a weirdo
Can tha call 'em that these days? Weirdos?

THE PAINTER

He drank alone, just a couple,
checked his pockets for change,
found it fell short.
He heard the landlord say *See you later*
for the last time.

A gentle giant, not quite fifty,
striding in the night air, almost home.

He'd spent his life
in streets like these,
spent his life trying to paint them –
not like a photograph
but as he saw them now,

teeming with life
all the way back
to the days of horses and carts -
strange abstract work
he couldn't sell.

Striding in the night air, almost home,
a gentle giant.

They were in the shadows,
four cheeky lads, asking for fags,
saying *come on, Mister*.
They'd been drinking, having a laugh,
smoking some skunk.

Almost home, a gentle giant.
Called him *a mean old cunt*,
landed a sucker punch,
knocking him off his feet
and out of time, flat out
in the path of a car.

A gentle giant,
gone by the morning.

PERCHANCE

In a slapped hard stupor
with dirty feet

pushing a plough
behind four farting mules

in a field alongside
an electrified fence

at the border
between have and have not

The Nation's Favourite Poems

NORMAN WRITES

You open it, and take it in – it's like
being attacked in broad daylight,
pinned to a wall by a red-faced adolescent
suffering a delusion of omnipotence.

It's no letter, it's a sermon, and if
being preached to by an angry nutter
was something you welcomed, surely
you'd have joined the Southern Baptists.

It pisses on your good humour, ruins
your plans – not very grandiose plans
it's true, but all the same something
you'd been looking forward to for some time.

WILDLIFE POEM

Taking a smoke at the open window
I spot a big spider, big enough anyway
in a web in the top corner. I love wildlife,

I feel passionate about its preservation,
but I need to mess with spiders
for the horror they've brought into my life.

I blow the smoke straight up at the spider
who gets giddy, falling onto the windowsill,
walking round in circles like a guilty cardinal.

An easy target now. Wish I still had a cat –
Josie gobbled spiders every chance she got.
She chewed with a sour face, legs dangling from her mouth.

ROBERT MITCHUM

Although fans such as I
would argue that numerous films of his
are the sort of films everyone should see,

asked one time which of them
he liked the most, he laughed and said
Hell, they pay me to make 'em, not watch 'em.

Too much podex osculation
going down in Tinseltown to suit Bob.
He wrote wild poems and smoked grass all his life,

paid the LAPD a grand a month not to bust him.
He once rescued Charlie Parker from a dustbin
and he never got too big for his boots.

HEY THERE

How come you find it acceptable
to watch quiz shows all of a sudden?
There's a simpleton's grin on your fat face –

aren't you paying attention or what?
You scaled Masada once like a gazelle,
now look at you. You're there in your dim room

like a cobweb, like a cup of tea
gone cold. You're there like a bongo
no one ever bangs a rhythm out on.

You remain baffled by the world at large
despite the facts you now love to reel off
such as naming the moons of Uranus.

AFTERNOON WITH DAVID

When I turned the corner and spotted him
smiling in the sunshine in his garden
with a cup of tea at a white plastic table

I became unsteady, thrust out a hand
moving sideways more than forward
all in the gasp of a shock then over

and he said 'hi' quite cheerfully
as did I, then sat down across from him
and accepted a brew and piece of cake

and sipped and chewed, marvelled at his laughter
and the fight he was putting up
beneath a parasol as the sun died.

ANOTHER FINE MESS

You spent last night with eight comrades
and two coppers, if that stoned type was right
about one in five at any meeting of lefties.

Well, he should know. He looked crazy enough
to play the flute, or write for a living, crazy enough
to sneer at a judge from the dock.

You were scoffing fish 'n' chips by lock gate six
when things went BOOM! You were burnt black, hairless,
rendered quite deaf, and you lost your sense of humour.

Do something to help me! wails Oliver Hardy
down the years, his hopes sinking, his ear
full of milk, his legs tied round his neck.

1970S BRITISH BLUES

Punching the same ragged riff half to death
the tuning all over the place
he just knew he'd never impress anyone. So

he did a Pete Townshend, which was a hoot,
and taught himself instead to drink eight pints
without losing control of the pool table.

One hot summer he was chased by coppers,
caught in woods and given a fair kicking.
Like but not like a hire purchase agreement.

'Man Who Dug Golf Course Up Had Taken LSD!'
gushed the headline of the *Chronicle*
after the magistrates finished him off.

TRIO

He'd be trying to save a butterfly
from a slow death at the bathroom window,
she'd be hanging washing out on the line,
the cat parading round her feet.

That was summer. In the winter
they'd be side by side on the settee,
the cat snoring softly in his lap,
poets and house painters calling all hours.

When rain was belting down, a freezing wind howling,
the cat would stand and stare, furious in the doorway,
before turning to look at him or her as if to say
Are you going to do something about this or what?

AUTUMN LOVE POEM

She was coughing again
last night, I couldn't sleep

and sat at our table,
nervous in the moonlight.

Something at the window
was trying to get in,

the moon looked right through me
and made a hollow sound.

The moon once sang and danced,
once told the greatest jokes;

my girl laughed for ever,
my girl and I both laughed.

I'll make some soup, good soup,
stir honey in her tea.

Her clothes hang loose, slip down.
She filled them in the spring.

HEART

Two nurses came, wheeled her away;
the lift door opened, she waved a thin hand,
they went in, disappeared

and I
sat there
with nothing

to do
except
sit there

and time
sat with me
barely

breathing
un
til

I crouch at her bed-side
clutching a mug of tea
she sips from through a straw, flat on her back.

She's off somewhere
with the morphine, wild-eyed.
'Isn't it nice when they like cheese!' she says.

VISITING

When will they cease poking
'n' prodding my darling?
She's had enough. I've had enough.
Better days better be coming.

I tell her Chester's gorilla was seen
bursting his britches again,
lugging a large amount
of rhubarb and lager,

and I missed a bus by seconds
and had to wait for half an hour
at the stop across from
the Freemasons' dive.

The lights were on.
I could detect movement
behind the frosted glass.
It was silent, the whole street was.
No one joined me at the stop.
No one said hello.

BLUE FROGS

She had bony fingers
that held a syringe
she used to inject ink
into frogs.
The bloated blue frogs
looked flummoxed,
wobbled round
for a minute or so
before dropping dead.
She laughed and smirked
and laughed and shrieked
and laughed and whooped.
It was a heavy thing

for a little boy to take in.
He watched her stoop
to pick the dead frogs up
one at a time by one leg,
drop them in the dustbin.
He watched her go inside,
shut her door.
He sat on the stone steps,
stared round.
Small pools of ink
dotted the yard.
If he shut his eyes he saw
blue frogs as statues.

66, 67, 68

That year booting a ball
against the panelled steel door
of the post office garage
the great clanging, rippling racket
as the ball whacked against it
all the way to bedtime
Moore to Charlton to Hurst WHACK!
what a bloody goal
that one crossed the line alright
no one ever told you to stop
no one bothered you at all.

*

You were put in a uniform,
waved off to boys' grammar school.
Part of the uniform was a daft cap,
to be worn like a flag of surrender
from leaving home to arriving at school.
Prefects were stationed at odd parts of town
and if you were caught with no cap
you'd be given cap detention,
an hour of writing
'I must wear my cap when travelling to and from school'
over and over.

*

Master of air guitar
Anyway, Anyhow, Anywhere

and other glorious rackets
alone at last, in your room
out of the poxy uniform
after the torture of the day
lurking about all evening
trying it on with Maria V
who half-fancied you because she said
you resembled one of Strawberry Alarm Clock
who you thought were all foul.

BIRTHDAY GIRL

When I sat down
and wished her a happy birthday
she said birthdays
were nothing to celebrate,
they just reminded you
how much time had gone
and how little was left.
Perhaps she guessed
what was coming –
all the good times done with,
packed away like old hats –
drinking herself senseless
in an absence of fun.

That day, on her thirty-second birthday,
we sat in the sunshine
as tiny birds
hovered round us,
landed right next to us
making a fine racket,
as if demanding an explanation,
or offering one,
if we could only understand.

BOTTLENECK

He went to a very dark place
his wife tells us, her face like chalk,
and stayed there till the day he died.
We try to picture Pete in his dark place.

A pint or two with Nev before the train
becomes a load of pints and fuck the train.
Remember this, remember that, remember…
It was over thirty years since I last saw Pete -

just the three of us Nev, we were blotto,
we smoked all the hash through a bottleneck,
lay trapped for hours like turtles on our backs.
And watched the sky unzip its cool leather jacket.

RHINO

His door slams shut like a head butt.
He's growling like some beast in a trap.

You creep to the peep-hole, see him lurching
beneath thick rolls of electrical cable.

He's told you more than once he works away, Scotland,
yet every day he's in and out like a rhino.

Once at midnight you stood in this same spot,
watching him crawl along the corridor

drunk as can be, swearing all the way, then
the prolonged agony of the key and the lock…

He has a line of vehicles in the car park.
They're always there. Never in Scotland.

LOVE STORY

It was hard to resist
when he read her message:
Get your arse over here
my ashtray needs emptying.

Seems he was forgiven
for the comments about her dad,
for what remained of her Audi,
for maybe everything.

Come here Darlin', he said,
taking her in his arms
before tripping, straight through
the plate glass living room door.

RED WINGS

They were arguing
well no, not even that
just arsing about

but it ended with
Frank's forearm sliced open
down to the bone, elbow to wrist

blood spouting
in all directions, the flesh flapping
like two red wings

a pale witness
throwing up all over
everybody's feet.

IF

If all music sounded like the world's angriest hornet amplified a
    thousand times
and if "wheat" did not appear on every packet in our kitchen but
    "trilby" and "vest" did
and if 'My Funeral' was a popular name for a girl
and if dodos weren't extinct but sailors were
and if magpies recited poems in the voice of Noel Coward
and if David Icke was wrong about the lizards
and if Captain Kirk and Mister Spock materialised every time you
    looked in your wardrobe
and if a cat running up a curtain was the basis for the world's most
    popular religion
and if Picasso had died a virgin in a house full of tears
and if people bought so many books they had nowhere to put them
and if pork pies and tobacco turned out in the end to be good for you
and if all the stupid films were brilliant films
and if the Marx Brothers had been called the Hitler Brothers and
    their reputation had waned
and if thoughts and ideas weren't lost if you didn't note them but
    waited for you in the fridge
and if the Prime Minister replied to questions with harmonica solos
and if the moon landings had never happened, or had
and if there was more than one way to outrun a lion
and if the strings of your heart could not be plucked
and if we encountered the under toad at an early age and knew when
    he was coming every time
and if Professor Hard Times and Joe Ignorant were the Trotsky and
    Stalin of British politics
and if 'Once Upon a Time in the West' was set in the East
and if everybody had size fourteen feet

and if a cat running up a curtain was a vital clue
and if the Queen published a lurid sex manual
and if an old school tie was merely something you used to choke a
    bastard
and if we all had to hide in a foreign embassy for ever knitting
    patterned pullovers
and if coming second was better than coming first
and if it was only possible to speak in the present tense
and if no one could ever miss a bus, or catch an undertone
and if people working in fish 'n' chip shops were better off than lawyers
and if you could stare at a boot and find something in it and not just
    a foot
and if we were immortal and God was an abandoned pizza with a
    cigarette crushed out in the crust
and if people still had lives rather than gadgets
and if Tarring Neville was not a village but a procedure
and if Peter, Paul and Mary had been called Dick, Balls and Quim
and if no one spent their life looking for stuff to sniff at
and if *Beat the Devil* was not a movie liked only by phonies et moi
and if kicking against the pricks was a degree course at Oxford and
    Cambridge
and if President Oscar Flake made smoking marijuana compulsory
and if a postcard from the seaside was a portent of doom
and if the world's most venomous snake was a pacifist
and if a cat running up a curtain was a cure for cancer
and if the greatest minds of our time all chose television game shows
    as a career
and if birds could only fly backwards and were constantly colliding
    comically
and if ashtrays could be used to replace diseased lungs
and if bicycles were poems and saddlebags field recordings
and if game birds enjoyed being blown to bits in mid-flight

and if you always got a good night's sleep no matter what
and if investment bankers always spoke with their fingers stretching
        each side of their mouth
and if Malcolm X had been white and Bob Dylan had been black
        and still only one had survived the 60s
and if Thelonious Monk was still gigging at the Five Spot
and if one and one made boo and boo and boo made boo hoo
and if something bit you on the leg every time you travelled by train
and if hamsters surprised us by saving the planet
and if the ghosts of Frank Zappa and Bill Hicks were running on
        the Republican ticket
and if Vincent Price and his mother were there to greet us at the
        gates of Paradise
and if a cat running up a curtain was an ingredient in a pie
and if the lines of a poem could be read in any order
and if it was impossible to run out of steam
and if the second world war had been a hen party
then maybe this would be the nation's favourite poem.

IN A HOSTEL

He forgets
his medication
sometimes,
came to this place
for a month
without it.

'It stops me
from wanting
to kill people,'
he says
from the next bed
with the lights out.

Lonely as a Crowd

NEARLY TIME

It's nearly time for face masks
to be worn at all times by everyone.

It's nearly time to speak
in a false voice, warm and friendly.

It's nearly time to accept
no gifts, or be as lost as you can be.

It's nearly time to bury
your face in your hands behind closed doors and weep.

It's nearly time to milk
your dying cow for all it's worth.

It's nearly time to eat
slices of dry bread like a thief.

It's nearly time for truth
that persists like the sky and the screaming.

It's nearly time to spit
on cherished dreams and their dreamers.

It's nearly time for noises
that glow in the night.

It's nearly time to crawl
through mud in the name of the Lord.

It's nearly time for the wolf
to rise from his grave and collect everything he's owed.

It's nearly time to hold
your breath and cross your fingers hopefully.

It's nearly time to think
of the perfect retort and say it again and again.

It's nearly time for a demijohn
to be the must-have fashion accessory.

It's nearly time for the sun
to start to wax and wane.

It's nearly time for Death
to suggest it had all been a mistake.

It's nearly time to acknowledge
you didn't laugh because you weren't sure it was a joke.

It's nearly time for something real
that cannot be denied.

It's nearly time for God
to find Himself in a giant egg cup, a giant spoon poised above.

It's nearly time
to dip a soldier.

I'M GEOFFREY

My dad's nocturnal adventure
with a packed suitcase and muddy bare feet
includes getting picked up at a bus stop
by a young woman in a transit van
who took him to her place, fed him and washed his feet
before handing him over to the police.

*

I'm sitting round with my brothers.
Clear signs of dementia. We can't
be thinking he might get better. He could
burn the house down, good God

now he doesn't know who I am.
Says I look a bit like his eldest son, Geoffrey.
That's me, I tell him, I'm Geoffrey.
Don't talk daft, tha too old.

*

My Uncle Bill was no uncle, just my dad's pal.
He dropped dead in the pub while playing pool,
forty-seven. He was wearing a suit and tie.
My dad's standing with him in the garden,
laughing in the sunshine at the same old stories.

IN THE SPRINGTIME

The queue outside the Aldi
spreads all round the car park,
out onto the street and round

the corner where it meets up
with the queue at the bus stop
like a couple on an awkward first date.

I count fifty more or less
socially distanced would-be shoppers
ahead of me, then lose the count.

One person leaves the store,
trolley piled high with pasta,
baked beans and biscuits,

another is waved in by a black girl
with a gap in her front teeth
just like mine and Jimmy Tarbuck's.

A Nigel Farage thinkalike
in front of me turns round
to give me his version of things,

which goes on and on
as the shopping body shuffles forward
like it's not well, forty minutes

and I can only console myself
that it's sunny, no rain,
and I won't live for ever.

Finally I get there, exchanging gaps
with the black girl, finally I'm in there,
but only to find the shelves all but bare.

Some fat git on his mobile:
'It's absolutely mad Susan,
there's not a single chip in t' place.'

No beer, no wine, my God, just the hard stuff,
not much of that. A bottle of dark rum
catches my eye, wins me over.

There are bog rolls across the road
in the newsagents, I overhear,
but not by the time I get there.

HOME AT LAST

The fortieth day of my house arrest.
I fall asleep so easily – not once
have I got through 'Murder Most Foul'.

I sang the phrase "Well, the" hundreds of times
day after day for a week. I got dead good at it.
I'm working on "danger on the rocks" now.

*

It seemed a bad time to visit A & E
but it was deserted. I was the sole patient,
limping along the gleaming corridor like a three-legged dog.

I have to elevate my foot, sit with it up
till it gets better. Which should be a few weeks.
Which will pass like decades of misery.

*

Oh to be in a hot country,
guzzling moonshine on a ganja plantation,
an honoured guest, welcomed

for my knowledge of polyrhythms
and the poetics of alienation
and loads of other fibs.

NEIGHBOURS

Him with the tattoos and weekend children –
once told me he used to play in Bad Seeds
and still gets Christmas cards
from Nick Cave – they're bundling him
cursing into a police van,
a couple of the coppers dripping wet.

Her with the daft old dog and winged glasses
says it's the funniest thing she's seen in ages.
They walked up to him – "You're nicked!"
Then he shoved them in the canal, just like that.
They landed in the middle of all these ducks,
flapping their arms and screaming blue murder.

Going up in the lift
with her with the bald patch
who doesn't have it now
I hear it's all about drugs,
a burglary at the Chemist's.
I don't say I believe her, I don't say I don't.

On the third floor
the smell of weed
almost knocks me out.
'I hate that smell,'
says her with the bum-brushing ponytail,
'if I'm not part of it.'

THE EFFORT

He wakes slowly
from a dream of childhood,
a dream of strength
and a sense of purpose,
a dream full of wishes
that might come true,
plans for tomorrow
and the day after.

He sits drinking water
and not smoking a cigarette
at three o'clock in the morning.

He once stopped for two days
but it was a mistake –
he ran out of money
in a hostile city -
had to hitch a lift back,
making small talk
as his head spun
from the effort of not smoking.

He sits scratching his chin
and not smoking a cigarette
at four o'clock in the morning.

The guy behind the wheel
had said, *Howdy, partner,
I'm from Austin, Texas,*
and started banging on

about armadillos,
whose vile eating habits
include a taste
for maggot-ridden flesh.

He sits tapping his fingers
and not smoking a cigarette
at five o'clock in the morning.

THIS FLAT

This flat is where music comes home to chill,
where clouds fill the windows with great notions,
this flat is where light gathers and dances,
where herons and kestrels and owls say Hi.

This flat was made to be paced in deep thought
and to resound with the gift of laughter,
the perfect place to stand and say out loud
'Who cares what a bunch of nitwits might think?'

This flat is a top spot to get blotto,
to greet the crack of dawn with a good swig,
this flat is like a poem fighting to live,
to get out there in the world and frolic.

WINTER LOCKDOWN BLUES

Amber warning, heavy snow, sub zero.
Nothing to do but climb the wall, listen to something low.

Full white car park, part buried cars, spots of movement.
Dogs in bright coats, a scaredy cat, wrapped up humans.

I hope there's plenty to eat in the house.

A young woman, maybe twenty, striding along.
Blue jeans, red vest, sandals, mane of black hair

stuck to her back. She couldn't be wetter.
She looks good, (did I take my

seven o'clock tablet?) psychotic but good.

Sometimes I get so desperate I recollect
something in me tired of turning the other cheek.

TOMORROW NEVER KNOWS

I dreamt I was Ringo Starr's mate,
dishing up beans on toast
all hours of the day and night –

Ringo, I said, am I losing my mind,
or have we in fact been taken over
by an alien species?

Sometimes a dream continues on another night.
I'm hoping that's the case with this.
In my favourite dream, the one where

I have absolute power, Boris Johnson Night
has replaced Guy Fawkes Night
and the firework displays are dead feisty.

NO COMFORT ZONE

Pressure is now the norm, we're under it always,
even fetching supplies can end up touch and go.

I feel old, take my time, heavy bags in each hand.
A youth on a doorstep sneers and spits at my feet.

A few facial repairs required just for starters.
Only three teeth left now and they don't meet.

My snore, I'm told, sounds like a death rattle
at the bottom of a deep pit.

Twenty years since I did anything to shout about.
Charity shops are where I exist now.

I yearn to fry an egg and a slice of white bread,
smother them in salt and get stuck in.

WIZENED

Wheezing like a wizened ex-miner
on the cold streets of South Yorkshire in the '60s –
why are the hills so steep? They never were before.

I find my friend in his usual chair.
He sits whittling on the same piece of wood;
it goes nowhere and will always arrive.

He's a heavy drinker, compulsive gambler,
terrible womaniser – he'll admit it, adding
he's got his faults as well of course.

He doesn't mind religious folk
if they don't mind him. He knows the Joke Police
are cracking down; his lips remain unzipped.

LONELY AS A SHROUD

Simply to limp along
like a half-starved stray cat
all the way to the bottle bank

can feel like a triumph
after waking from a nightmare
of Karen Carpenter on a slab in the morgue,

her bare-knuckle take on 'Barstool Blues'
breaking hearts from a last legs jukebox –
you never saw anybody deader.

You love the racket when bottles shatter,
chucking them in one at a time,
your face a mask, man in control.

LONELY AS A CROWD

The Trump's pompous, petulant face
coldly peering as I chew my corn flakes.
He says his ratings are out of this world,
or did he say ravings? I say he did.

I was trapped for some time last night
with a highly-rated saxophonist
who fell hard for the one about Ornette Coleman
taking a razor to his balls. A gullible nitwit,

full of himself and thick and misogynistic.
"What a knobhead!" I heard one woman say,
in fact it was my wife. "What a total - "
Highly-rated. Big fat white guy. Sold out.

MOSTLY BOB

It must be strange to be so close
to retirement, and still not know
what you want to be when you grow up.

At least you've got old Bob, young Bob,
middle-aged Bob, all the Bobs
to help you with the long dark nights.

I know it's not just Bob, but it *is* mostly Bob.
There's no need to sulk, it could be far worse.
It could be a much bleaker scenario in many ways.

So you went to the doctor's and you're OK?
You're OK except for your heart?
No, not your heart, your brain?

HATTER'SLEY

Someone offering to set fire to you
for next to nowt, someone raising money
for bloody dogs, a catalogue of disasters

waiting to occur, all the way from bowel cancer
to losing your marbles, eating 'teasted toecakes'
for breakfast, keeping your collection of beermats

and matchboxes in a 'boardcard box',
signing your name with an apostrophe
in front of the s and feeling smart for doing it.

Your wife hands you a list and you walk to the shop.
You are required to purchase, just in case of emergency, bacon,
and you can see the wisdom of that.

MONDEGREENS

Not elegant trump
elephant gun

Not that fried egg feeling
that Friday feeling

Not her favourite psychopath
cycle path

Not Josey Wales
save the whales

Not hey typical
atypical

Not pig-faced angular rough shark
squid

SMART PATCHES

Goodbye toe fungus
hello holiday homes

a Japanese scientist has discovered something
frozen pies

reduce your wrinkles
get rid of turkey neck once and for all

this is the place where germs will thrive
beautiful Asian women want older men

primer and foundation
shoes to conquer the world

Japanese smart patches
before you go to bed

MICHAEL GOES MISSING

Six months after you were thrown out of art college
you stayed on this Balearic island
for more than a week, less than a month,
there was a hippy artists colony there,
out of their heads from all the hash cookies
they munched on continually, sculptors and painters
and what have you, music generated
by large windpipes catching the breeze
and the surf's relentless rhythm.

Then there was Istanbul, hiding there
in the world's shittiest hotel.
There was Karachi, the worst meat
you've ever had in your mouth in your life.
There was a giant pan, burnt black, steaming.
India was more like it, in the streets
people were everywhere making music.
You bought some bongos, yoghurt and a flute.
You could see things, smell things, something in you

breaks apart then reassembles smartly,
you hitch a ride in a very small car crammed with carpets
and you get all the way to the Bulgarian border
and the driver doesn't have the papers for the car.
You know this is crazy. That first night
you sleep in a pumpkin field, and you wake up
and there's a guy pointing a rifle at you.
What am I doing here? you ask yourself.
You could well be the first black man he's met.

You're here for saying no, I shall not kill
Vietnamese people for you.
It's not a joke but seems kind of funny.
You look up and see the pale moon
hanging on for dear life.
They're talking about walking on it soon.
You take a breath. 'Hey, can you speak English?'

COMING CLEAN

I'm too honest for my own good
which is why I lie all the time
and why everyone knows I lie
and no one thinks I'm not lying
nor do I pretend not to be lying
therefore that's not really a lie
if it's so transparently a lie
so yes, that is, no no, I did not lie
and if I did I didn't know I was
except when I did, but listen
I'd be lying if I told you
there are people out there who believe me
and there are people out there who believe me
believe it or not and I put it to you
truth, lies, what's the difference
I am a man of honesty, integrity
a true lie for every occasion, mm
bear with me, I had my hair trimmed for this
I just need to lie about a few more things
before I go, not that I'm going anywhere
I am who I am and should be
rightly adored.

WAREHOUSE

My dad would be shaving
by five; I'd shaved
the night before.
I'd make a pot of tea,
sit hands round mug
in my blue overall.

We drove to work
in silence, more or less;
he was hard-of-hearing
from the steelworks -
fifteen long years then just like that
no more steelworks.

In the army
he'd driven officers
from A to B, still had the air
of that driver.
He kept his eyes on the road,
smart remarks to himself.

Now seen as a good worker,
moved up from the warehouse
to operations planning.
When we got there, walked through the door,
he'd disappear down his hole
and I down mine.

SPACE

It's not true that people like me.
OK, it's true sometimes
but mostly not. They don't like me
and I often can't stand the sight of them.

To be with my wife is enough for me,
just to occupy the same space.

She's engrossed in *The Invasion*
which is, she claims, a cracking read
about the gentrification of working class areas.

What gets her most is the indifference.
I think at times that gets me most as well.
Times like today, yesterday, tomorrow.

WHAT NEV DID NEXT

Unpublished

BROKEN SLEEP

He indicates with open palm
a vacant seat at his table
Even though my legs are broken

I opt to stand, drunk in shorts and a vest.
"I never thought I'd win!" he says loudly.
Not one person in the place could care less

My wife turns over in her sleep.
I place my arm around her waist
and my thighs against her buttocks

but it's hot and sweaty and I soon move
softly away and lie flat on my back,
my chest conversing with itself loudly.

THIS TIME TOMORROW

I'll be sixty-seven

and the fresh face

of the new Labour MP

for Selby and Ainsty

will make me feel like

digging a hole, hiding.

Dylan's Shadow Kingdom

will arrive right on schedule,

sound great in the afternoon sun.

I'll place a photo of

my old friend Mark on the side so

he can dig it with me.

BREAKFAST WITH BABS

When he gets up in the morning
she's in her gown at her oven,
poaching two fillets of fresh fish

and asks if he wants some breakfast.
"Yeah!" he says, starving, taking a spot
salivating at her so posh table.

"OK," she says, "I'm off to put on my
suit and armour, leaving in ten,
do yourself some toast or something."

Then she takes the fish from the pan
and places them in two pink bowls
for her two fluffy white pusscats.

MILNER'S WAY

Milner liked a disagreement,
always found a way to come out on top.
I remember him telling me

first impressions were rarely correct,
you should always give a person
a second chance.

"I don't know about that, Milner," I said,
"I'd say first impressions
are usually spot on."

"To be honest, Geoffrey," he said,
"the first time I met you
I thought you were a right arsehole."

SHOVE YOUR SCOTCH EGG

There's this Olive Oyl lookalike,
I see her all the time in the village centre,
legs like twin poles in tight leggings,

swigging from a can of lager,
arguing at the top of her voice
with some part of herself

or else sitting still as a pin ,
si lent, staring, spooky
with wild hair tied in braids.

I've talked to her, and she to me,
she taps roll-ups, and one time
I offered her a Scotch egg.

GROUNDHOG DAY

Life is too short

to watch this silly film

for what seems like

the thousandth time

yet here I sit

watching this silly film

for what seems like

the thousandth time.

ALWAYS SOMETHING

There's never enough time,
always something waiting
to use you up —

a dripping pipe,
a hammer and a box of nails,
dirty dishes in piles,

an automated voice droning
followed by the star key
till you're sure you've gone mad,

scraping up what's left
of your cat from the road
while passing drivers grin.

LIVING LEGEND

You don't bump into a living legend

every day, but here comes the one

who stinks of shit from yards away,

walks like his pants are full of it,

a slow, awkward zombie shuffle.

I say hello and he

mutters something

but I'm not sure he knows who I am

or even who he is.

Something he once told me:

When they demolish his house, they'll find

bodies in the chimney, half a dozen.

CLOCKS

The clocks go back an hour tonight,
which means an extra hour of sleep,
or' would if he could get to sleep
without a drink.

Only a week - it seems
more like a month more like two months.
He fidgets in his chair
like a bald man waiting for a haircut.

If only the clocks
went forward a month!
He'd feel justified drinking again ,
after having gone all that time without.

SIX BOTTLES

He couldn't help but notice

Bargain Booze

were two hours' late

opening

Old Peculier
The Legend
6 bottles
Are enough

Maybe, he wonders

as he falls backwards

into the waste bin

maybe more than enough

IN THIS DARKNESS

Tired of lying
in this darkness
like a potato in a field.

He feels sorry for the Israelis,
he feels sorry for the Palestinians,
he feels sorry for the whole human race

and it's making him ill.
He'll have to stop.
Feeling. Sorry.

In his tired head he makes a two-word poem,
'The Mexican Janitor'·
Jesus swept.

BURGLAR ALARM LENSES

A mental bread and water sort of job

the machine running on automatic

all you do is pick up the moulds

after they tumble down the chute

you put them on the table to cool down

then you pack them in Standard One boxes

one hundred and thirty lenses per box

in ten rows of thirteen

each row separated by a piece of

corrugated cardboard

every minute seems like ten

a whole shift is like four days without sleep

you imagine you're trapped in a bubble

where the normal laws of time don't apply

you shout to people outside the bubble

but they seem not to hear you or see you

you know there is a place out there

where you can sit, forget all this

you just have to hang on a few more hours

you just hang on

WAREHOUSE AESTHETICS, 1975

The only teenager
in the smoke room
I smoked and overheard
the conversations of my elders—
cars, football, the telly—
boring stuff. One day however
a passionate debate
with raised voices broke out
on the relative merits
of large or small tits
on a woman Most of the men
belonged to the bigger the better
school of thought
but the smaller tit advocates
argued their case well.

LOCKBRIDGE WAY HAIKU SOCIETY

Ken's tireless ghost roams
the building, looking for faults,
walking stick tapping

Dawn arrives, bringing
the song of the reversing
orange fork lift truck.

A dustbin man shrieks
See the size of that bastard!
sounding quite girly.

The police cruise round
the car park and are soon back
to do it once more.

Three dogs tussle for
a flattened plastic football ,
growls filling the air.

The black and white cat
finds a good spot in the sun
to worship itself.

IN THE NIGHT WITHOUT A MASK

Sometimes I find myself
sitting at this table

the middle of the night
just the darkness and I

the only time
tears might run down my cheeks

tears for everybody
all the people, even myself

but then the sun comes up
and I fasten

my brave and hopefully cheerful mask
back in place.

MISTER DEATH

I met the grim reaper
when I was twenty-six,

he stood with his head bowed
at the foot of my bed

but I wasn't ready to go with him
and made that pretty fucking clear.

Now there's no sign of him
yet I sense him

creeping up behind me
but when I turn round quick

he's made the movement too,
a real sneaky hide-behind type of bastard.

EASY LIVING

Enjoy those long days of summer
In a Deluxe Zero Gravity Chair

S,t comfortably, stand up less painfully
Tell the time even when it's dark

Make your armchair smarter
The humane and harmless way

Make a,r frying even easier
Tread safely at night

Remove impurities hygienically
Hear with perfect digital clarity

One spray kills instantly
As sensuous as a caress

THE ANTIDOTE

Mingus Mingus Mingus

Mingus Mingus

good and loud and Joyous,

half a dozen

cans of good stuff

in his stomach,

a dozen more

still in the fridge.

He needs these days

of drink and music

to forget

the job, the grind, the slow dying,

the wrong-headedness

and jokes that die

before they're born,

the polystyrene cups

lifted to awful lips

and the smell of burnt plastic

everywhere.

Both his hands were

covered in blood,

a small puddle

formed on the floor

He sat and bled

while some twit

decided it didn't

need stitches

and was back on the job

within fifteen minutes.

WHAT NEV DID NEXT

Tall as ever, seeming even taller,
Nev looks down at poor little me
and sits and starts to talk, and I talk too.

He says he can still see the real me
I'm not sure who the real me is
but I'm glad Nev can still see him

The day flew by, over so soon.
It was great to see Nev but not so great
to say goodbye, not that we spoke that word.

One minute he was there, then he'd gone,
shut the door behind him. What Nev did next
is something I guess I won't ever know.

CONTENTS

#

66, 67, 68	455
1970s British Blues	449

A

About Something	191
Acquaintance	147
Act	62
Action	426
After	427
Afternoon with David	447
After the Stupid Film	416
Against Suicide	265
A House with Bare Floorboards	83
A Huge Bag of Potatoes	140
Alex	229
Alive Not Dead	409
All Weekend	368
Almost Unbelievably	46
Almost Unbelievably	282
Always Something	501
Another Fine Mess	448
Arthur's in Grimsby	433
A Terrible Song	218
A Terrible Song	339
At This Table	214
At This Table	338
Autumn Love Poem	451
A Week	162

B

Bad Attitude	230
Bad Attitude	346

Because	11
Because	276
Before And After Breakfast	198
Before and After Midnight	210
Bernard's	406
Big Turtle	254
Birthday Girl	457
Blue Frogs	454
Boss Arse	237
Boss Arse	350
Bosses	145
Both Liars	163
Bottleneck	458
Boys' Grammar School:	14
Bravo	148
Breakfast with Babs	497
Breathless	413
Briefcase	51
Briefcase	288
Broken Sleep	495
Bruise	169
Bruise	328
Builder	144
Burglar Alarm Lenses	506

C

Captain Value	192
Carte Blanche	37
Chicken Bone Charlie	241
Chicken Bone Charlie	351
Chicken Cashew Nuts	370
Christmas Shopping	274
Christmas Shopping, Sheffield	43
Clocks	503
Cold Spot	200
Cold Spot	334

Coming Clean	489
Cowboy	224

D

Date	152
Days	285
Dear Friend	395
Death's Boots	112
Death's Boots	314
Desert	55
Desert	283
Diary Of A Week In September	279
Dishwasher	168
Domestic	77
Don't Lean On The Sideboard	380
Don't Worry	97
Don't Worry	306

E

Easy living	511
Eccentric Hair	308
Eccentric Hair	93
Elsecar Reservoir	103
Elsecar Reservoir	310
Encounter	119
Eternal	113
Expecting to be Homeless	422
Experience	117
Eyad's Cassette Tape	171
Eyes, Lips, Miss	91

F

Factory, Late Seventies	*15*
Fatty Fairholme's Gang	411
Fingerprints	81
Five Years	92

Forever Changed	78
Foreword	7
Fortune Cookie	402
Frank O'Hara Five, Geoffrey Chaucer Nil	36
Future Games	47

G

God and Bananas	183
Good Day in the Lab	393
Grace	149
Grace	318
Grey	88
Groundhog Day	500
Grumpy	425

H

Half Deaf	127
Half-Time	34
Hannon In A Nutshell	305
Hannon in a Nutshell	84
Harmonica	209
Hatter'sley	484
Head of Steam	434
Heart	452
He Dreamed He Burst Balloons	355
Hemingway in 10 True Sentences	429
Her New Biker	215
Her Place	151
Her Question	217
He was certainly an intellectual	27
He Was Certainly An Intellectual	273
Hey There	446
His Chilling Thought	213
His Fault	398
His Fingernails	248
His Fingernails	354

Holy Air	154
Holy Air	319
Home at Last	472
Home Video	176
Hot Glue	253
Hours	35
How it Went	186
How She Puts It	52
How She Puts It	287
Humphrey Bogart	226
Hyphen	102
Hyphen	309

I

I Did Brain Surgery On A Barnsley Pub Floor	246
I Did Brain Surgery On A Barnsley Pub Floor	353
I Dreamed I Burst Balloons	257
If	462
I'm Geoffrey	469
Impious	401
I'm Putting on Weight, Last Year's Trousers	38
In A Heatwave	264
In a Hostel	465
Infamous	391
In Phil's Butchers	110
In Phil's Butchers	312
Instead of an Alibi	424
In t' George	435
In the night without a mask	509
In the Room and Out the Door	385
In the Springtime	470
In This Darkness	505
It's Sunday	44
I Was an Unarmed Teenager	197
I Was an Unarmed Teenager	333

J

Jerome K. Jerome	105
Joy	233
Joy	347
Jumbo	199
Jupiter	185
Jupiter	331

K

Knife	431

L

Lee's Dog	238
Like Harpo Marx	243
Lingerie on a South Yorkshire Clothes Line	94
Living Legend	502
Lockbridge Way Haiku Society	508
Lonely as a Crowd	482
Lonely as a Shroud	481
Looking Hard, Feeling Mean	379
Loomings, 1984	23
Love Poem	21
Love Poem	284
Love Story	460

M

Man Enduring Heatwave	371
Manuscript Discovered Behind a Bathroom Tile	177
Massacre	167
Master of Ceremonies	428
Meaningless Incident	143
Meatballs, Jerusalem, Tattoo	290
Meeting Hudson	121
Memorable Afternoon at the Cinema	247
Men Without Clothes	114
Michael Goes Missing	487

Milner's Way	498
Minus Three Point Six	304
Minus Three Point Six	80
Mister Death	510
Mondegreens	485
Moon	25
Moose Face, Wobble and Plonk	378
Mostly Bob	483
Motions	420
Mucky	32
My Shoes Need Cleaning	205

N

Nearly Time	467
Neighbours	473
Nervous Before Breakfast	139
New Thing	419
New Year's Morning	20
Nineteen Eighty-Four	405
Nineteen or Twenty Pigeons	211
Nobel Prize Poem	307
Nobel Prize Poem	86
No Chance	227
No Chance	344
No Comfort Zone	479
No One Knows Why	407
Norman Writes	443
Not California	126
Not for Aesthetic	155
Not For Aesthetic	320
Nothing Nothing Nothing	258
Not Pretty	261
November	157
November	322
Numbered	150

O

Ongoing	245
On the Buses with Dostoyevsky	146
On the Buses with Dostoyevsky	317
Our Monica	262

P

Party People	394
Pathological	82
Perchance	441
P For Poem	267
P For Poem	358
Pieces for Three Wooden Blocks	69
Piper	159
Piper	323
Piper Again	170
Poem for Billy	141
Poem for Kylie	399
Poem Mentioning Adolf Hitler	234
Poem Mentioning a Sweeping Brush	179
Politics	175
Politics	330
Portrait	31
Posh	249
Powder Man	225
Powder Man	343
Praying for a Miracle	124
Pretty Funny Things	362
Problems with the Overflow	76
Problems With The Overflow	298

R

Race Relations on the Shop Floor	239
Randy Newman et al	208
Readers	277
Reckless	129

Red Dungarees	252
Red Dungarees	357
Red Wings	461
Refused Water	106
Remembering Dennis's Eyes	108
Remembering Dennis's Eyes	313
Rhino	459
Ride	231
Robert Mitchum	445
Rum and Blue Sky	189
Rum and Blue Sky	332
Rump Poem	397

S

Scared	54
Scared	136
Scotching The Seagull Rumour	377
seven in the morning.	160
Sex	29
Shadows on the Beach	19
Shadows On The Beach	278
Sheep's Brain	33
Shoulders	24
Shove your Scotch egg	499
Singing	49
Six Bottles	504
Sixteen At A Time	361
Six Ways to Say O.K.	181
Slaughterhouse	63
Slaughterhouse	299
Sleepless	263
Sleepless	356
Small Chocolate Heart	219
Small Chocolate Heart	340
Small Man in a Small Town	366
Smart Patches	486

Smoke	201
Smoke	335
Snapped	386
Snowballs, Italy	56
Sofa Factory	255
Sofa Factory	359
Something from a Stupor	165
Something From a Stupor	324
Something Unfixed	130
Space	491
Spider	57
Spider	292
Spliff	232
Splinter	204
Splinter	337
Split Shift	17
Spock's Brain	120
Stand-In	364
Star Guest of the Day	90
Still Grinning	180
Stockings and Slippers	373
Stop	137
Straight	184
Straight, No Chaser	423
Stuck With It	421
Stupid Stuff	365
Summer Sick Note	228
Summer Sick Note	345
Sunday Western	193
Sunrise	381
Swamp Music	128

T

Ten Hebiums	388
That Was Your Life	367
That Weekend, You Wore	30

That Weekend, You Wore	275
The 41 Greatest Lists of 41	206
The Ankles	190
The Antidote	512
The Barking of Stray Dogs	173
The Barking of Stray Dogs	329
The Bootleg Series	71
The Chickens	166
The Chickens	327
The Cigar	12
The Confrontation	396
The Depth	221
The Depth	342
The Drummer	50
The Drummer	291
The Effort	474
The Fat Man in Paris	67
The Game	408
The Guitar	250
The Handshake Poem	244
The Handshake Poem	352
The Joke	18
The Last Time I Saw Ernest Hemingway	89
The Laughing Face	118
The Man at Number Ten	45
The Man At Number Ten	280
The New Boy Hears Good Advice in the Toilet	14
The New Mr Barnsley Something	135
The NEw Right	28
The Next Break	363
The Next Move	111
Theology	22
Theology	281
The Only Son at the Fish 'n' Chip Shop	115
The Only Son At The Fish 'n' Chip Shop	315
The Painter	439

The Persuaders	131
The Persuaders	316
The Phone Call	251
The Plan	212
There's Not Much Fish in a Fish Pie Is There	403
The Saxophonist's Eyes	53
The Slacker	202
The Visit	116
The Visit	188
They Were Both Liars	325
Things Suddenly Liven Up	242
This Flat	476
This Time Tomorrow	496
Threatening At Any Moment To Blush	289
Three Mornings	85
Tin Bath and Scary Hole	410
Toast	286
Tomorrow Never Knows	478
to start a new life with.	125
Town	161
Trio	450
Trouble	302
Two Bombs Are Better than One	109
Two Boys, Three Fish, and One Dad	414
Two Hours and One Minute	222
Two Love Poems	203
Two Love Poems	336
Two versions of a Cartoon Strip	240

U

Under Strict Orders	369
Unrecalled Melody	216
Unshaven Poem	372
Untitled, Kibbutz, Late Seventies	66
Untitled, South Yorkshire, Mid-Eighties	98

V

Visiting	453
Volunteer	158

W

Waiting For It to Die	432
Warehouse	490
Warehouse Aesthetics, 1975	507
What I'm Up To	430
What Nev Did Next	514
When You're Pushing Fifty	375
Whining, Cascading	122
Wildlife Poem	444
Winter Lockdown Blues	477
Within These Walls	39
With the Bosses	266
Wizened	480
Woman's Tea Party	142
Working Through	374
Worksongs	40

Y

Ye Merry Gentlemen	404
Y'Know Warramean?	235
Y'Know Warramean?	348
You Don't Dream At All If You Can Help It	392
You're Not Even Funny, Not Even Smart	74

LAY OUT YOUR UNREST

www.ingramcontent.com/pod-product-compliance
Lightning Source LLC
Chambersburg PA
CBHW031748220426
43662CB00007B/318